T0079726

Pavol Frič et al.

Czech Elites
and General Public:
Leadership, Cohesion,
and Democracy

UNIVERZITA KARLOVA V PRAZE
NAKLADATELSTVÍ KAROLINUM 2010

ISBN 978-80-246-1844-9

Contents

Introduction

Pavol Frič

Many believe that today's globalized world is moving toward unification and a single global society. In spite of that, individual countries, societies, and regions are obviously very different from one another. For instance, they have met with varying success in the international modernization race, coping with the global crisis, or getting involved in the global division of labor. Hardly anyone would deny the fact that a society's success in competition with others depends on the ways its people's collective decisions are formulated and the interaction between its elites and ordinary citizens. Crucial for success is whether or not elites lead the society well and whether or not citizens follow them willingly, with a high level of trust. Using today's fashionable terminology, one may say that a good elite-public relationship provides society with an indispensable kind of social capital. The quality of the relationship strongly determines the society's future.

The idea of writing a publication about the relations between the Czech elites and the general public resulted from our work on a team project entitled, "Modernization and its actors",[1] which views elites and the general public as actors of modernization processes within the Czech society. Therefore, post-communist social modernization provides a general framework for our studies of elites and the general public in all chapters of this book. While individual authors apply their own perspectives to the "catch-up modernization" (Habermas) in post-communist countries, the requirements the current stage of

---

1 The team project is part of the research project entitled, "Visions and Strategies for the Development of the Czech Society Within the EU", funded from the Research Program "Development of Czech Society in the European Union: Challenges and Risks" at the Faculty of Philosophy and Arts and the Faculty of Social Sciences, Charles University in Prague, grant No. MSM0021620841.

modernization places upon elites and the general public create a common ground for all texts. This means that the authors combine the institutional and normative approaches to studying elites in their texts. On one hand, they analyze quantitative data based on a positional definition of elites and, on the other hand, their analysis relies on the reputational definition of elites. While the institutional dimension of elites forms the ground for elite identification, it is not analyzed in detail. The formal and objective aspects of elite members' positions or careers (the current position in the hierarchy of power, the methods of recruitment, preparation, qualification, social demographic characteristics, social origin, political background, etc.) are not central to the analysis. Instead, the issue of elite quality or, more specifically, the quality of elite-public and intra-elite relations, stands at the center of the authors' attention. Elite quality is seen as a relational phenomenon, arising out of elite relations with other elites or the general public. Therefore, all chapters share the "relational approach" to the study of elites. For that purpose, the authors analyze data from parallel empirical surveys of representative samples of Czech elites and the general public. All chapters rely on comparing the answers to the same questions between the different elite types or between elites and the general public. The juxtaposition of elite/public opinions, attitudes, and behavioral indicators upon the background of different theoretical concepts of elites and democracy forms the core of all chapters.

The common methodological and conceptual framework is complemented by the more-or-less explicit effort of all authors to address the issue of democratic stability in a post-communist society like the Czech Republic. In Chapter 1, Pavol Frič and Aleš Bednařík investigate the elite-public relationship as one between leaders and followers, who should be fulfilling the "task of their time" (Ortega y Gasset) and face the requirements of levelling off with the West and democratic functioning. The authors understand leadership as an attribute of "genuine elites" (Sartori) and focus their analysis on the leadership potential of Czech elites. Chapter 2 by Pavol Frič and Martin Nekola analyzes elite cohesion using the network analytic concept of elite structural integration (Higley, Hoffmann, Kadushin, Moore). The main theme revolves around the "elite central circle", whose democratic/oligarchic character is tested on empirical data for each elite segment. Chapter 3 applies a similar approach using the concept of "elite consensus" (Field, Higley). The author, Milan Tuček, tests the level of Czech elite consensus by comparing the opinions of different elite segments to the current situation and future orientation of Czech society. In Chapter 4, Libor Prudký addresses the question of what level of value consensus between elites and the general public (and one among the different elite segments) is available to support social cohesion in society as a whole. In doing so he uses Inglehart's concept of "materialist/postmaterialist values". Finally, Chapter 5 by Martin Nekola uses the concept of "political support" (Easton) to investigate elite and public preferences pertaining to aspects of representative and participative democracies as forms of political regime and power sharing between elites and the general public.

All authors investigate the elite relations with other elites or elite-public relationship in order to identify structural factors of sustaining or jeopardizing democracy in a post-communist society. Their findings are rather disappointing. In short, the Czech elites have very limited leadership capital and the elite central circle is clearly becoming increasingly oligarchic. The fact that the Czech elites have a general consensus on democratic rules and the country's future orientation is a result of their situational pragmatism, rather than shared value orientations. While members of the general public declare high democratic support, their value orientations continue to be affected by state paternalist, egalitarian, and xenophobic attitudes. This prevents Czech society from reaching the ideal of an open democratic society. The general public does not make a courageous follower of its elites and many citizens are longing for a strong leader to put an end to elite parasitic and predatory behavior. These findings suggest that the future of the Czech post-communist democracy will not necessarily resemble one of the several democratic models we know from Western Europe. Instead, it may in a relatively short time take a specific form of "leader democracy" (Weber) with populist "plebiscitary leaders" bringing strong Caesarian elements and turning the masses into a "spiritual proletariat". The future of the form of leader democracy is made even more likely by the fact that the Czech Republic is not the only Central European country heading in this direction. Similar tendencies have prevailed in Slovakia for a long time and have clearly become more prominent in Poland and Hungary.

1. Leadership in Czech Elites

Pavol Frič and Aleš Bednařík

Introduction

The relationship between phenomena like elites and leadership was noticed and conceptualized by the very founders of elite theory (Pareto, Michels, and Weber). In this chapter, we will link the two phenomena based on the principal assumption that the elite-public relationship to some extent is, or should be, one between leaders and followers. We thus depart from the general assumption that elites fulfill "the function of leadership" within society (Kaminski & Kurczewska 1995: 137) and the general public fulfills the function of followers. We also assume that a moral right exists to demand that elites act as leaders. Here we build upon the classical elite theory's normative premise that elite positions should only be assumed by "the best of the best", who also have leadership on their agendas. Clearly, all high-level functions in a given society cannot be occupied by the best people. We concur with Sartori that there are two possible types of positional or "altimetric elites": (1) genuine ones, who have achieved their positions through their abilities and merits, and (2) false ones, who have power without ability (Sartori 1993: 144–5, 170). Genuine elites, sometimes referred to as authentic or natural, represent the "aristocracy of talent" (diZerega 1991). They are extraordinary people who excel in their qualities, education, skills or charisma (Hoppe 1992). Such characteristics lend them natural authority and respect in people around them. They are "natural sovereigns", leaders of people around them. Leadership can therefore be seen as one of the attributes of genuine elites. Just as we have the right to demand that genuine elites take up elite positions, we also have the right to expect that genuine elites lead the people around them. Elites must be comprised of leaders in order to be followed by citizens (the public) voluntarily. Otherwise, they would have to use violence to only temporarily ensure their elite positions. Classical elite theorists knew that long-term governance cannot build on violence. In short, elites must bear leadership qualities in order to maintain authority.

Every person has some leadership potential and can put it to work as they want, insofar as circumstances allow. We are of the opinion that a formal elite position gives better chances for leadership qualities to show than the position of a normal member of society or an organization. An elite position in the society's institutional structure gives the individual a unique opportunity to prove himself a leader. Therefore, we find elite positions to be ones of leadership. A person holding such a position should act as a leader, or else they are blocking the position from another person who could potentially use it to realize their leadership potential. On one hand, some people in real elite positions are unable to lead and, vice versa, some individuals who are not holding elite positions act as informal leaders. On the other hand, we take a generally applicable assumption that an elite position implies a leadership role to a much greater extent than an ordinary position. This is yet another reason to expect elites, i.e. all people in high functions, to act as leaders.

For a long time, social scientific studies of the leadership phenomenon focused on the specific personal or professional qualities of excellent individuals holding leading positions in politics, the military, the economy, public administration, etc. From this perspective, leadership was seen as an autonomous phenomenon that is owned by individuals as the result of divine intentions or training combined with practical experience. Social scientists long hoped that by studying high numbers of leading personalities they would be able to identify a set of qualities that "makes one a leader". Any person with such qualities was deemed "predestined" to become a leader. However, as it turned out, no such set of qualities exists, and therefore, it is impossible to predict who will and who will not become a leader, or establish that a given person is a suitable leader in any situation or social context. Recently, leadership research has been increasingly dominated by the relational construct of leadership, i.e. one that also includes followership. The relational perspective builds consistently on the seemingly trivial fact that only a person who has followers can be deemed a leader. Once leadership is seen as contingent upon followership, it can be conceptualized as a process in which a leader not only gathers and leads his/her followers, but also followers choose, accept, and legitimize their leader. Leadership and followership are increasingly understood as phenomena that constitute each other (Collinson 2005). Metaphorically, they are two sides of the same coin. Joseph Rost (1993: 191–192) emphasizes that leaders and followers should be studied as a whole because they have a single relationship, their goals and activities are one, common, and shared. Another proponent of the relational approach, Edwin Hollander, finds the source of the mutual dependency of leaders and followers in a process of exchange between them. In this process, both leaders and followers give and take, expect and receive, and are required to do some things and able to provide others. It is a complex and reciprocal process. The interaction is understood as two mutually dependent reciprocal systems forming one single system (Hollander 1993: 30). Both systems are equally important. The necessity to view followership as equally important has been increasingly popular in contemporary leadership research. More and more attention has been given to the leader-follower interaction and the process constituting leadership. Interactional, transactional, or transformational models of leadership, collectively understood as relational approaches to leadership, has been in the field's focus and, at the same time, has been adopted by the authors of this text. John Antonakis provides us with a typical example of the relational approach to leadership by defining it as an influence process that occurs between a leader and followers in a given context (Antonakis 2006: 6). This emphasis on context is not accidental and arises from the widely accepted fact that leadership—or the leader-follower relationship—does not exist in a vacuum. It rather takes place in a specific situation that influences the relationship and leadership efficiency. The specific situational context, as studied in the relational approach, constitutes of more than just the historic background, the current level of societal, community, or organizational development (technological and economic achievements, institutional, social, and demographic structures, etc.) It is primarily constituted by cultural patterns, deep-rooted notions of authentic leadership in elites and the general public, perceptions of elite leadership style, and accepted leadership traditions reflecting the collective identity of leaders and followers.

The relational approach to the leadership/followership phenomenon is based on the premise that leadership goes beyond leaders and, analogously, followership goes beyond followers. Leadership embraces followers as well as leaders. It is primarily something between them. Leadership and followership constitute mutual dependency and the nature of such dependency is indicative of the quality of leaders and followers themselves. Both the leadership and the followership concepts include certain notions of leaders and followers. This, however, does not make these two concepts identical or interchangeable. The leadership/ followership concepts stand for a complex, reciprocal social system in which leaders and followers fulfill different roles. Leaders and followers bear different, yet interconnected and complementary, roles that make the behavior of a certain collective or social group efficient.

The goal of this chapter is to summarize the available empirical evidence on the extent of Czech elites' leadership capital and the kinds of leaders Czechs prefer. We are going to build primarily on the results of four quantitative surveys conducted by the Center for Social and Economic Strategies, Faculty of Social Sciences, Charles University in Prague (CESES) during the past six years. The first, entitled "Elites and Modernization", was carried out in winter 2003/4 on a sample of 826 members from five basic elite segments: political (143 respondents), economic (152 respondents), administrative (173 respondents), media (169 respondents), and cultural (189 respondents). We will refer to this survey as "CESES 2004". The second survey, entitled "General Public as a Modernization Actor", took place in autumn 2005 on a representative sample of 2300 Czech Republic citizens aged 15–79 using stratified random sampling with a 70.3% response rate. This survey will be further referred to "CESES 2005". Third, a field data collection entitled, "The Elite-Public Relations", was done in autumn 2007 on a sample of 1035 respondents in high formal positions within political (111 respondents), public administration (138 respondents), security (77 respondents), economic (260 respondents), media (97 respondents), cultural (arts, education and research, churches, 158 respondents), and civic sector (204 respondents) institutions. This survey will be referred to as "CESES 2007". The fourth survey, named "General Public as a Modernization Actor II", was conducted in autumn 2005 on a representative random sample of 2353 Czech Republic citizens aged 15–79, and will be referred to as "CESES 2008".

Since the views and attitudes under investigation are relatively stable, we believe that the different times of data collection for the respective general public and elite surveys is not an important source of bias. Our data analysis was based on the premise that every person holding a leading position faces the need to fulfill a leadership role. In other words, all members of the general public and elite members' subordinates expect elite members to fulfill the leadership role. Elite members must take into consideration the fact that their elite status is assessed and evaluated from that perspective. Therefore, we will attempt to apply the relational approach to leadership in our data analysis. The same sets of questions have been answered by both the elite and the general public samples. Therefore, we are going to confront the views expressed by elites and the general public in order to identify the leadership capital and leadership style preferences. The evaluations, opinions, and attitudes of elites and the general public will be compared for the different leadership parameters. With certain caveats, we will study public opinion as a test of the existence and effects of Czech elites' leadership capital. At the same time, we are aware of the fact that the available data do not cover these topics comprehensively. In some cases, the data are illustrative, rather than fundamental. This means that some findings will necessarily be interpreted with caveats or in slightly ambiguous ways.

1.1 What is the leadership capital of Czech elites?

Several decades ago, Ralph Stogdill stated in his review publication on leadership that the number of leadership definitions is almost as high as the number of definition authors (Stogdill 1974: 259). Unfortunately, the situation has not improved since then. Some authors conclude that leadership simply means different things to different people and there is no need to ask what should be generally understood under the terms "leadership" or "leader". The authors of this chapter reject the latter opinion and believe that a general foundation for understanding the leadership role can be identified, at least in broad terms, in order to differentiate the leader concept from related concepts such as manager, boss, superior, ruler, or sovereign. Beyond that, we assume that such a general fundamental meaning of leadership applies to all situations and circumstances. In other words, every person who is fit to be labeled a leader must under all circumstances fulfill several basic, leadership role-specific criteria. Relevant literature often describes the ideal role of a "genuine" or "effective" leader. There is an affluence of detailed accounts of the ways real leaders acted throughout history; the functions a leader must fulfill in order to be efficient in a given community, organization, group, or team; and the things one must do in order to be considered a real leader. Furthermore, there have been numerous attempts to reduce, organize, or categorize those accounts in order to make the leadership role more easily understandable. If we continue in this direction and apply the principle of Occam's razor to the past attempts, we may reduce the leadership role to the basically invariant fundament that may be expressed in three words: *vision, change, and mobilization*. These three words encompass the core leadership agenda and provide benchmarks for assessing individual leadership qualities or leadership capital. The relational approach to leadership makes one's leadership capital contingent upon the ways his/her abilities are seen by followers. The leader's abilities as perceived by followers may enhance or weaken his/her leadership qualities. One who is perceived as a weak leader tends to have little leadership capital and his/her leadership is bound to be weak in reality, and vice versa (Dowding 2008). In our text, we will understand leadership capital as a set of elite member leadership qualities along with the public (follower) perceptions thereof, in terms of offering an attractive vision, achieving the envisaged change, and mobilizing followers. There are three basic leadership qualities:

(a) providing an attractive vision,

(b) finding a suitable way of achieving the change envisaged, and

(c) mobilizing followers in order to achieve change.

The leader's ability to apply his/her leadership capital in specific situations is one of the basic preconditions of successful leadership (Stout 2006). Leadership capital may be invested carefully, or wasted by not respecting existing circumstances impact on results. Elites' leadership capital is bound to be little if they do not understand or refuse to understand what kind of role they are supposed to fulfill at a given stage of societal development. A functional coherence between the nature of elites and the role required of them by the current situation in society is extremely obvious in transforming societies. Here, elite agendas change quickly, according to the development stage a society has reached, and this leads to changing elite identities and types. For instance, Jacek Wasilewski (2001) distinguishes the following three developmental stages of Central European post-communist societies:

(1) transition, during which elites take strategic decisions about regime change,

(2) transformation, characterized by very specific ways of building democracy and market economy, and

(3) consolidation, in which a new order is stabilized and works smoothly.

Wasilewski argues that specific elite types are required in order to manage each of the three developmental stages: the elites of transition, transformation, and consolidation. The following Table summarizes Wasilewski's three-stage model.

Table 1.1: The role of elites in three developmental stages of post-communist societies

Elite type	Main agendas	Mass-elite relations
Elite of transition	– dissociation from state socialism – vision of a new order – democratization	– symbolic politics – high elite autonomy – mobilization of masses in the name of a vision – elite moral legitimacy
Elite of transformation	– detailed program of political and economic reforms – implementation of reforms	– reform politics – restriction of elite autonomy, professionalization of politics – re-mobilization of masses
Elite of consolidation	– consolidation of democracy, economic efficiency, and growth – inclusion in the global division of labor – European Union integration	– distributive politics – further restriction of elite autonomy – interest institutionalization – gradual demobilization of masses

Source: Adapted from Wasilewski (2001: 137)

While we find Wasilewski's three-stage model compelling, we believe it is outdated because the development of post-communist societies is past the consolidation stage. New agendas are facing the relatively consolidated democracies and economies of these countries. The project of new regime consolidation should be followed by a new project in order to further develop these countries. While the consolidation has oriented them towards pro-Western modernization, the concrete outcomes of this process remain unclear. Findings from our surveys demonstrate, on one hand, that the Czech elites share with the general public an ambition to level off with the West, i.e. reach the level of the most developed European Union countries; on the other hand, neither elites nor members of the general public know exactly how to accomplish this (Frič 2003).

What does it mean to level off with the West? What is the task of our time[2] for today's elites? Following Wasilewski's model, we may raise questions about what the ongoing "levelling off" stage should look like. In what ways is it different from the previous consolidation stage? Answers to these questions must be sought on the background of modernization theory. Most proponents and protagonists of this theory share the opinion that developed Western societies are currently finding

---

2   We refer to Ortega y Gasset's idea that each era in the development of a society has its own fundamental task or mission which elites should recognize and fulfill (Ortega y Gasset 1923).

themselves in a stage of transition from industrial to post-industrial societies. Clearly, much less shared are opinions about the nature of the post-industrial stage and how its existence can be identified. Abundant time has been spent inventing names and concepts for such "new societies"—such as the technetronic society, the information society, or the knowledge society[3]—where research and development based changes in production technologies propel development. As a result of current modernization developments as well as critiques of the modernization theory—mostly focusing on its alleged blind progressivism, scientism, and technological determinism—contemporary modernization theory has been increasingly oriented towards social or civilization-cultural factors of modernization processes such as traditions, competition between nations and institutions, the institutional framework of modernization, value and normative systems, civic culture, or social cohesion. Such reorientation made us realize that the existing post-industrial stage of modernization (the third wave, the late modern) differs from the industrial era in a series of changes beyond technological development. These changes primarily affect the goals, subject, method, and time-space mode of modernization:

(1) *quality of life,* rather than material wellbeing, is emphasized as a goal,

(2) the modernization of social institutions, patterns and rules in society's life—the socio-cultural modernization—comes side-by-side with the development of production technologies, capacities, and management,

(3) modernization changes are a result of a *reflexive process* in the society as a whole, rather than mere decisions by industry leaders and government policy makers. Such a process includes everyday criticism, debate, and negotiation among diverse social actors, including civil society actors, and

(4) the international modernization race has become a *global* one, in which a society's position depends on its integration into the global division of labor, rather than an ability to produce for domestic market.

The country is supposed to level off with the soft, socio-cultural side of modernity, which is essential for further development and economic applications of science and technology. Given the above accents of contemporary Western modernization trends, the "levelling stage" of development in post-communist societies, as a follow-up to the Wasilewski model, should have the following characteristics:

---

3   Miloslav Petrusek provides a comprehensive review of "new society" concepts and theories in his *Societies of the Late Modern Age* (Petrusek 2007b).

Table 1.2: The role of post-communist elites in levelling off with the West

Elite type	Main agendas	Mass-elite relations
Levelling elite	– developing deliberative democracy – building an efficient and accountable public administration (fighting corruption, clientelism, and exclusion) – providing access to law enforcement for all	– modernization politics – transformation of masses into a genuine public – expanding the opportunities to participate in decision making – partnership, mobilizing the public as a policy actor

Clearly, priorities for levelling off with the West must be sought in the economic and technological domains as well as the socio-cultural domain. However, economy and technology are not the primary agendas in respect to the shared ambition to level off with the West. The choice of societal modernization priorities depends on elite and public preferences. It is essential that we know what priorities are preferred and make sure these priorities are subject to public debate.

1.1.1 Ability to provide an attractive modernization vision

Direction setting is normally considered one of the leadership attributes. Only a person who sets the direction of collective action can be a leader (Tucker 1981). A leader shows to his/her followers the way that must be taken in order to succeed in their collective effort. That is why the leader must stand out, be "the frontman", someone followers can clearly distinguish and walk behind. A leader is an attractive role model, a pioneer who hews out the path through an unknown terrain in order to reach the desired destination. At the same time, followers require information about where the leader is taking them and want to make sure they will not drag their feet or go in circles. A leader gives a sense of direction (Keller 1980, 270) to followers by formulating a vision of the future that is to be accomplished collectively. That is why there is no leader without vision. As Robert Terry says, "vision is the heart of leadership" (Terry 1993, 38).

Clearly, a leader should show the direction to others by being an example, yet this is usually not sufficient to attract followers and keep them. Followers expect to be told what their leader wants and what is at stake, they want to know the meaning of their efforts. They want to see the picture of a desirable future and how to achieve it. Thus, a leader should conceptualize, clearly formulate, and communicate this vision of the future to (potential) followers so that they can identify with it (share it with the leader). The vision followers are identified with is then incorporated into the leader-follower relationship as an essential element of collective identity. Such a vision energizes followers and focuses their attention on a desirable future.

It is normally good news for modernization if a country's elites and general population agree on the view that countries ahead of them should be caught up with. Unfortunately, the Czech Republic exemplifies the fact that such an agreement may bear little relevance for the way a country tries to level off with developed countries. Only 20% of the general adult population and 24% of Czech elites believe that this might be accomplished within the next ten to fifteen years (CESES 2007 and 2008). Why do Czechs have so little confidence? What is the reason of their skepticism? The media and citizens themselves often seek the answer to these questions in their elites' poor leadership qualities.

Socio-cultural modernization may be the result of interaction among blind market forces, or that of purposeful activities of social actors, including elites and the general public. It is usually subject to strategic efforts by a large number of policy actors from the public, commercial, and non-profit sectors. The leading role of elites in this respect is clear. The principal task of elites as socio-cultural modernization leaders is setting modernization goals and providing the vision of a modern society towards which they want to lead their followers—and which can become the subject of followers' rightful demands. An overwhelming majority of leadership theories find vision formulation an essential part of leadership capital. However, the general public and even the elites themselves largely question the existence of a vision of Czech society's further development.

Most citizens (60%) and elites (62%) agree that the Czech Republic lacks a vision to be followed by most people.[4] On the other hand, the formulation used admits that there are several visions of social development in the Czech Republic that elites might be trying to get majority support for. Indeed, people do not want to have a single dominant ideology over their heads. They rather want several visions in order to be able to select one common vision (this opinion was expressed by 60% of respondents). The democratic competition of visions seems more acceptable than a "dictate" of one vision. At the same time, people's answers suggest that, so far, there is nothing to choose from—they are not living in a plurality of social development visions competing for

---

4   Sources: CESES 2007 and 2008.

their attention. The general public feels the necessity for new visions. Old visions are discredited or morally outdated and the reproduction thereof gives rise to cynicism rather than excitement. However, elites rather avoid providing new visions for a post-industrial future of Czech society. The general public in fact claims there are no visions to debate in the Czech Republic. Paradoxically, our time is "obsessed with the future" (Milén 2002: 177) but lacks visions people would take as their lead. As early as 1989, Jürgen Habermas decried a total lack of innovative and future-centered ideas (Habermas 1990: 4–5). In an affluent society, quality visions of the future are scarce.

When elites are unable to persuade the general public of the necessity to follow a certain vision—or when they do not have one—the effectiveness of cooperation between these modernization actors declines rapidly. With vision-free elites, it is not clear who leads whom: is the general public led by the elites, or vice versa? Elites often adapt to public opinion or take their lead from the subconscious desires of masses. Even if they have some useful visions, it is not clear to what extent they are shared by their followers. It is a well known fact that only a leader-follower consensus makes leadership sustainable in the long-term perspective. Therefore, the question arises whether elites and the general public share a consensual vision for the future of Czech society and, more specifically, its modernization. Such a vision need not be complex. A general idea without clear-cut details is sufficient. What is the content of this vision? Do the elites and the general public have corresponding ideas of the ways contemporary modern society in a European context should be shaped?

New emphases in Western societies' modernization processes resulted in the gradual transformation of these societies into a new developmental stage. Sociologists have begun to discuss emerging post-industrial, information, knowledge, or late modern societies. In order to study the possible realization of the Czech ambitions to level off with the West, we must know how this new trend affected the picture of a better, modern society that exists in the minds of the Czech elite and general public. This trend did not go totally unreflected, especially in Czech elites. However, elite and public visions of a modern society resemble, in many aspects, the picture of an industrial "smoking chimneys" society, rather than those of the information or knowledge societies. The general public typically emphasizes material wellbeing and technological development. Both elites and the general public are little interested in civic activism and the global dimension.

Table 1.3: What do you imagine under the words "modern society"?

N = 826/2300, percentages*	General public	Elites
A society where people's material needs are secured	27	14
A society with a high quality of life	20	22
A society with developed institutions	19	34
A technically advanced society	17	20
A society integrated into global structures	1.4	1
A society with intensive civic activities	0.4	1
Other	16	8

* Proportion of the given option in all valid answers.
Each respondent chose three answers.
Sources: CESES 2004 and 2005.

The elite-public agreement on the ambition to level off with the West is not accompanied by a corresponding vision of the kind of modern Western society everyone wants to level off with. In short, neither the public nor elites have an adequate idea about what contemporary modern society should look like. While unable to provide a vision of modern society as integrated into the globalized world, elites are better off in their relation with the outer world in terms of modernization. They are much more open to international influence[5] than the rather closed-up, cautious general public. In this respect, elites have a much greater modernization potential. How such a potential is used are a different question.

We basically cannot conclude that there is a full public-elite consensus about a modern society vision for the Czech Republic. Indeed, any such full consensus would be rather unhealthy. More importantly, those parts of the consensus that pertain to new modernization emphases are about neglecting, rather than supporting those new emphases. On one hand, elites have a broader perspective and a greater potential to fulfill their leadership role in social modernization. On the other hand, they are not sufficiently ready for this role. A significant part of elites wants to lead society to a well-functioning industrial society, rather than an

---

5   Two statements expressing the respondent's attitudes to world powers and foreigners, respecively (question 7h and 46a) were used to indicate openness to international influence. This operationalization was used to construct a new variable, representing a scale of openness/closedness to international influence. An auxiliary variable (PROVIN2) is constructed as an unweighted sum of answers to the two questions. The resulting variable (PROVIN1) is constructed as a 5-point scale that corresponds with the scale used for the above two questions. See Technical Appendix for details.

information or knowledge society. This means that they, along with most members of the general public, want to level off with the Western industrial past, oblivious to its post-industrial present.

1.1.2 Ability to find a suitable way of modernization change

Clearly, the better future that is facing followers in the visionary pictures formulated by their leaders cannot be accomplished without changing the existing situation. One who acts as a leading force of change[6] in society or their environment is a genuine leader. In Joseph Rost's words, "only when leaders and followers actually intend real changes is a leadership relationship possible" (Rost 1991: 115). A leader who merely pretends to struggle for change is not authentic. This does not automatically make every leader a progressive person. An envisaged real change may consist of innovation as well as a return to the old order. However, a leadership role is normally associated with (risky) innovation, as opposed to passive adaptation to circumstances.

Management and organization scholars often try to distinguish the roles of leaders from those of managers. One of the main differences is seen in the fact that leaders engage in fundamental changes to the organizations they direct, while managers merely apply standard patterns of business management. Notwithstanding the effort to differentiate between the leader and manager roles, one aspect that bridges both roles should not be omitted. It is a well-known fact that a good manager does not have to be a leader. On the other hand, every good leader must simultaneously be a manager. For instance, elite members with ambitions to become good leaders must not only persuade followers of their visions, but also find suitable ways of realizing them. They must realize or at least fight for them in a persuasive way. Leaders who fail to realize or fight for a vision become less authentic. A leader may prove to be a bad manager for the process of implementing the change envisaged, and thus become disqualified as a leader in the eyes of followers.

1.1.2.1 Hard or soft modernization

The Czech elites and general public share the ambition to modernize their society and level off with the West. This begs the question, how

---

6   Preventing change—e.g. averting a threat—that exists in reality or at least in the minds of members of a given society or community, also qualifies as change.

do they intend to realize such a change, i.e. what sequence of actions will help fulfill their ambition? Which way of modernization is right for us? Should we place stakes on "hard" modernization, i.e. inducing a swift scientific development and supporting technological innovation, or rather "soft" modernization of the ways institutions function, i.e. changing the rules and patterns of behavior and building a pro-innovation climate within society? This is not an easy decision. Ever since Karl Marx and Max Weber, social scientists have disputed the question whether modernization processes are propelled by economic and technological changes, or rather cultural, political, and institutional changes. To this day, social science has not provided a satisfactory answer to the economic-technologic/cultural determinism dilemma. The Czech elites and general public have solved the dilemma by supporting the third, easiest way of modernization—a balanced compromise between the technological and cultural orientations. Such a compromise solution seems to be rational, based on the idea that modernization has the best chance to succeed if technological and cultural changes are mutually supportive (Inglehart 1997: 10). Moreover, the compromise method of setting the country's development priorities conforms to the demand by modernization scholars that modernization processes are complex and combine the hard and soft orientations (Machonin 2000).

Table 1.4: Which orientation is more important for the Czech Republic's future success?

N = 2353/1037, percentages	General public	Elites
Orientation to science and technology development	29	38
A mixed orientation	48	48
Orientation to the development of culture, trust, and social cohesion	24	14

Sources: CESES 2007 and 2008.

The one-sided hard (technological) or soft (socio-cultural) modernization ways enjoy minority support in the Czech elites and general public alike. About half of respondents from both groups find themselves between the two opinion extremes, combining elements of both modernization systems.[7] The general public's more frequent

---

7   The technological, mixed, and social modernization dimensions are represented by a composite variable, TYPMO. Technical Appendix contains details on variable construction.

choice of the socio-cultural orientation is to some extent paradoxical because it should be the elites who lead society towards post-industrial society. Why is the one-sided soft modernization orientation so little represented in Czech elites? We know that the country's falling back behind the West during communism was mainly caused by sociocultural de-modernization (Cf. Schöpflin 1991, Machonin 2000, Machonin et al., 2001, Havelka & Müller, 1999). Logically, since we already have built a market economy and formal institutions regulating social life, we should be trying to level off with the West in the sociocultural domain.

1.1.2.2 Modernization models

To gather followers is an extremely difficult task unless ideas about the future are formulated in a single coherent vision, and even more so if leading personalities pursue competing visions, rather than speaking with one voice. This begs the question whether Czech elites as modernization leaders resemble, at least in broad terms, a leadership team, or rather pursue different ideas about the country's future that are not mutually supportive. The field of modernization models Czech elites are offering to society is highly dispersed, suggesting a rather low level of intra-elite consensus about future orientations. Even if the overwhelming majority of elites express support for the Western modernization model, their choice of model countries to be followed is extremely varied. Germany is the country most worth following for elites in general, and Ireland is the one for political elites. The list of countries named by Czech elites as models for the Czech Republic's further development mostly includes European countries (levelling off with the West is, in elite members' eyes, levelling off with the developed part of Europe), and in particular, the large countries at the core of EU integration. All in all, smaller countries in different parts of the world predominate among the model countries. Typically, elite members do not concentrate on one dominant country, and their preferences are greatly dispersed, and therefore, no generally acceptable foreign model for the Czech Republic's development can be identified. Germany and Sweden are most often mentioned as model countries, as respondents find them attractive for their strong economies on one hand, and "model" solutions of social security and health care on the other. The example of Ireland, the country most often preferred by political elites, indicates their higher sensitivity for actions within the EU (e.g. the use of EU structural funds), something Ireland has been very successful at. Countries of the post-communist world are clearly unpopular among the Czech elites. Only 3% (of those stating two countries) mention a post-communist country as their first or second choice, with only Slovakia and Slovenia are mentioned. As many as 88% (of those who stated two countries) choose European countries only, and Norway and Switzerland are the only non-EU members among those mentioned. New Zealand and the U.S.A. are mentioned among non-European countries. Almost half of respondents (46% of those stating two countries) choose a country with medium ranking population, i.e. similar to the Czech Republic. 70% of respondents mention a medium ranking country as their first or second choice. Almost half (47% of those stating two countries) mention a European, non-post-communist, medium-population country (Belgium, The Netherlands, Portugal, Austria, Greece, Sweden, Switzerland)[8] as their first choice. In conclusion, elites have some general idea about a model country: a democratic European country with a population size similar to the Czech Republic.

This idea is sadly insufficient as a modernization vision for Czech society. Capitalism is not the same everywhere in Europe. This fact is extremely important in terms of levelling off with the West strategically. However, it is either ignored by the Czech elites or, more probably, elites have not reached a sufficient consensus on international models for the Czech republic in order to support a focused strategy of imitating the more developed model. The international model for Czech modernization is extremely blurred. Rather than a strategic selection, this results in a chaotic effort following the motto "take a bit from everyone". It confirms the above hypothesis that not only do we have no one big vision of the future for most general public, but we also do not have a few clearly defined models (visions) to become subject of a meaningful public debate.

These, as well as the earlier-mentioned data, illustrate the relative lack of elite consensus on how to modernize Czech society. The poor elite consensus on modernization orientation might help explain elite inability to come up with a modernization vision that would attract a larger group of followers. Competition between visions and ways of realizing them in the Czech context is undermined by the existing crisis of prospective thinking in elites and the general public alike. Jan Keller (2001) offers another explanation for the absence of visions in the Czech political life by arguing that not having any vision at all is more favorable in today's fast changing post-modern world. Politicians find their "vision-free travel" around voters favorable because it enables

---

8   Source: CESES 2004.

them to react more flexibly to changing political situation, enhances their immunity from (voter or competitor) efforts to make sure their attitudes are consistent, eliminates accountability for betraying their own visions (and the ensuing risk of losing face), and expands discretion for backstage deals with political competitors. It is quite apparent that Czech elites do not act as a single open "leadership team". At the same time, the Czech Republic also does not have competition between two or several clear-cut modernization visions that would be supported by different parts (factions) of the elite.

1.1.2.3 A Czech way of modernization

The necessity of levelling off with other countries in the modernization race means that Czech society either gets better at modelling the most successful or finds its own shortcut, a Czech way to prosperity. The above data analysis suggests that the motto "the West is our model", is not as popular in the Czech Republic as it might seem from the shared elite-public ambition to level off with the West. Only a slight majority of the Czech general public finds efforts to reproduce Western modernization models meaningful. While most general public respondents agree with the necessity of converging with the West, they also share a provincial ambition to mentor the West. Most citizens believe that the Western modernization model may enrich the Czech Republic in some ways, especially in the socio-cultural domain. In other words, they say that the Czech westernization — copying Western modernization models — is necessary but we should manage it in our own, Czech way. While elites hold mostly similar attitudes in this respect, they are clearly more pro-western. At the same time, most elites view the West through the lens of their provincial self-centeredness, finding Western technological domination difficult to accept.

Table 1.5: General public and elite attitudes to the Western way of modernization

N = 2353/1037, percentages	Agree/Strongly agree	
	General public	Elites
Our reproducing Western countries' way of modernization makes no sense	41	31
Adaptation to the West is the only way for us to go	53	59
While more developed economically, Western countries might learn quite a bit from us	62	65

Sources: CESES 2007 and 2008.

Ironically, those Czech Republic citizens who, for the most part, confidently tell the West that economic development is not everything, simultaneously find cheap labor the most significant Czech contribution to the European Union (CVVM: 2004). In contrast, the more cautious elites primarily offer education, creativity, and spirituality to Europe (Frič 2005: 21). However, as suggested by their extremely fuzzy modernization model, elites are unable to "sell" such prominent qualities effectively, i.e. based on a streamlined modernization strategy for the Czech Republic. Therefore, the principal question remains open: whose offer is actually more realistic? What if the general public offering the proverbial "golden Czech hands" meets European demand better than the elites offering excellent brains? Who will better assert themselves in Europe — elites, or ordinary citizens? And are they able to assert themselves collectively when their ideas about the possible contribution to the EU are so different? The outcome is to a great extent revealed by looking at citizen and elite views of the Czech Republic's actions within the EU.

1.1.2.4 Which way of Europeanization?

The above answers of Czech elite members suggest that they view westernization primarily as adaptation to the European modernization model. Such a model is (to different extents) carried by the "old" EU member states. This means that Czech westernization includes solving the question of how the Czech Republic will strategically deal with its EU accession. How do the Czech elites and general public view such an "EU-ropeanization" of their country? Factor analysis has revealed three primary strategic orientations in the Czech elite and general public regarding the Czech Republic's actions within the EU.

First, a "provincial orientation" is most commonly represented. Specific strategies of a cautious guardian of national competencies, a defender of national sovereignty, and a protector of Czech business interests are developed on this background. The vast elite backing of the provincial orientation also explains their low support (34%) of EU federalization. As a "consensual" orientation of both elites and the general public, provincialism ranks as medium ambitious and the least open to Czech Republic's EU-ropeanization, echoing the outdated visions of a modern society isolated from the outer world.

Table 1.6: Role of the Czech Republic within the EU: the "provincial orientation"

N = 2353/1037, percentages	Agree/Strongly agree	
	General public	Elites
Try to acquire maximum possible competencies and a maximum possible share of decision-making within the EU	79	88
Primarily try to preserve its national sovereignty	84	81
Apply maximum possible government support and protection of Czech producers within the EU	88	85

Sources: CESES 2007 and 2008.

As the second most frequent strategic orientation of elites and the general public vis-à-vis the EU, the highly ambitious "activist orientation" emerges. It comprises two seemingly contradictory strategies: one of a rebel trying to liberalize the EU economy, in spite of the mainstream, and another of a specialist trying to adapt, seeking those EU policy domains where he would become indispensable. Both strategies are based on a high level of openness to EU-ropeanization, and are complementary. Within the general public, this strategy takes the shape of a non-conformist, rebelling attitude to the existing EU model. In contrast, elites also tend to rebel but more often tend to prefer the conformist "indispensable specialist" strategy. Political elites lean to the rebelling strategy more often than other elite segments.

Table 1.7: Role of the Czech Republic within the EU: the "activist orientation"

N = 2353/1037, percentages	Agree/Strongly agree	
	General public	Elites
Demand free trade with the whole world, not only within the EU	78	76
Focus on selected EU policy areas and become an indispensable specialist within those areas	51	61

Sources: CESES 2007 and 2008.

The third strategic orientation for the Czech Republic's role within the EU, which enjoys the least support, could be named "conservative" and minimally ambitious. Surprisingly, it comprises two different strategies. The first is one of a passive free rider who enjoys all membership advantages, but tries to contribute as little as possible. The other is an active strategy of an excellent member who always goes with mainstream EU opinion. From the EU-ropeanization perspective, these strategies may be minimally ambitious but, at the same time, they do not contradict the merits of EU-ropeanization. The public-elite comparison reveals that the conservative orientation is more often preferred by the general public, while elites wish to play a more active role within the EU.

Table 1.8: Role of the Czech Republic within the EU: the "conservative orientation"

N = 2353/1037, percentages	Agree/Strongly agree	
	General public	Elites
Invest as little as possible in EU affairs but make maximum use of available advantages and means	53	42
Go with the opinion mainstream within the EU and take diplomatic credit for being an excellent member	51	61

Sources: CESES 2007 and 2008.

Views of the Czech Republic's actions within the EU are relatively uniform across elite segments. Differences are statistically significant in two cases only. First, the "conformist and excellent member" role is most often supported by the political, economic, and cultural elites (~65%). Second, the "free rider" role (invest as little and take as much as possible) is most often rejected by the political, administrative, media, and cultural elites (~65%) and most often supported by the economic elites (64%).[9]

1.1.3 Ability to mobilize the general public

Implementing any substantive change or innovation in a society, organization, or community is, as a rule, a difficult task, as it faces resistance from those whose interests are actually or seemingly under jeopardy. Every social change brings about insecurity in those affected. A leader needs more than just a good vision and an innovative approach to change in order to overcome such resistance. In order to realize his/her vision and fight resistance to change, he/she must mobilize followers to engage in collective action strong enough to overcome resistance and achieve the change envisaged. Leader aspirations to "change the world" are quixotic without active follower support. Follower mobilization must be a fundamental part of the leadership role. James Kouzes and Barry Poster emphasize the importance of mobilization for leadership

---

9   Source: CESES 2007.

by placing it in the very center of their leadership definition. They understand leadership as "the art of mobilizing others to want to struggle for shared aspirations" (Kouzes & Posner 1995, 30). Every leader must more or less face the problem of "free riders" (Olson 1965), those who take a ride without contributing to achieving the shared vision. Free riders rely on others actively contributing to the desired change while they themselves take an effortless ride with them. Leaders thus face the problem of motivating and interesting followers in actively participating in solving problems along the path of change. They must constantly persuade followers of the necessity and rightfulness of collective action, pulling them into the process of change. Follower mobilization always takes place in a given social context, which may more or less facilitate or work against the change.

The leader-follower relationship is not one of bosses and subordinates. By definition, followers always have a choice (Edinger 1975). They should follow their leader voluntarily, as a result of informal authority. As Bowen says, while followers succumb to leaders, they do so voluntarily, based on their own persuasion. Leadership is "an interpersonal relation in which others comply because they want to, not because they have to" (Bowen 1974: 241). Warren Bennis and Burt Nanus emphasize that a leader motivates, rather than commands. Leaders lead by pulling others, rather than pushing them. They inspire, rather than direct (Bennis & Nanus 1985: 225).[10] Followers must trust their leaders in order to voluntarily obey their wishes and be persuaded and inspired. A decline in elite moral legitimacy in the eyes of the general public usually results in a loss of confidence in their ability to lead the society. The quality of the leader-follower relationship is traditionally indicated by the level of trust, and specifically in our case, trust in the different elite segments as expressed by members of the general public. We can say that the Czech Republic faces a reality of low trust in elite leadership abilities. Most respondents do not believe that elites are able to mobilize the public, are determined enough to modernize, or are willing to sacrifice for a better future for all. Most members of the general public do not consider elites to be leaders.[11] Their leadership capital is low because most potential followers

---

10 Once again, the thesis that one who manages may not be a leader comes up. For instance, elites may manage society without leading it. They may play the roles of "mere" managers of social happenings, without enjoying informal authority.

11 In order to illustrate young citizens' views of the political elite, we will quote two recently published contributions to a survey by the newspaper DNES. One was written by a business high school student, Martin Calada: "Our elite is, with few exceptions, a mixture of non-

within the ranks of the general public do not believe they have such capital. And since followers do not recognize leadership capital, they act as if there was no such thing, and therefore, according to the famous Thomas theorem, it does not exist at all. This means that Czech elites do not enjoy leader status with most of the general public.

The current situation in the Czech Republic is characterized by a lack of moral leadership. Abuses of public trust are seen everywhere, as exemplified by various corruption scandals of politicians, officials, soldiers, and policemen (the latter also suspected of organized crime links), financial fraud within banks and businesses, protectionism and clientelism in employment and public procurement, and all that is seen as elite failure in their leadership role. Elites who wish to mobilize the general public in the name of their visions must not only self-declare moral integrity, but also win public respect for their moral credit. The Czech general public is far from that. In contrast, it finds its elites selfish (72%) and corrupt — elites have worked their way up through acquaintances and corruption (68%). On the other hand, only a minor part of elites admit corruption (32%) or selfishness (36%) in their own ranks. However, most elites (59%) admit being too enclosed in a network of acquaintances and favors.[12] People who admit being stuck within clientelist networks can hardly be trusted to remain corruption-free. These negative views of elite moral qualities make them fatally disqualified from the leadership role. People with such a profile can hardly lead anyone anywhere.

On average, less than one-third of citizen respondents believe in elite leadership qualities. Half of respondents think that elites are unable to mobilize people in the name of a better future for all and are not determined enough to modernize the country. Most (69%) respondents do not believe Czech elites are willing to make sacrifices for the country's better future. Elites contradict these views and, above all, believe in their own abilities to mobilize people (84%). Elite confidence in their own ability to motivate the public is, however, undermined by their admitted inability to produce a vision that could be followed by most of the

representative and overpaid, often vulgar people who abuse politics in order to get rich, rather than changing society." Another contribution was written by education student Michaela Voráčková: "Our political elite is a disaster. I do not know why I should call these quasi-important gentlemen 'elite'. The laws they pass are useless. Laws that should be passed or considered are not on their agenda. Every party is bad in its own way. No matter which party we elect, we always choose the least evil one, instead of one that might lead the government rationally." (Co si myslíte 2007)

12   Source: CESES 2008.

society. Civic elites hold the most critical views of elite moral qualities (42%) and have the least confidence in elite ability to mobilize (79%) and lead the general public. In contrast, the most trust in elite mobilization capacity is expressed by administrative elites (88%).[13]

The general public provides a clear answer to the question why elites are unable to lead society: "Because they are corrupt!" This is indicated by a significant negative correlation between the ratings of ability to lead and elite corruption. And why are elites corrupt? Here the clear answer is: "Because they are isolated!" Both ability to lead ratings and elite corruption ratings are significantly correlated with the ratings of elite isolation: the more isolated the elites are found, the more corruption and less ability to lead the society is found. In conclusion, the Czech general public shows contempt for their elites, mostly does not respect their leadership authority, and tends to follow their negative example.

1.2 What kind of leaders do Czechs want?

Since the mid-1980s, social sciences have seen growing skepticism about the possible existence of individuals with universal leadership qualities for all situations. Concepts of socially constructed leadership have come forward. The social context in which a leader exists is often seen as a necessary condition for the existence and effectiveness of leadership. Long gone is the individualistic, economic-rational approach which assumes that leaders and followers are connected through their efforts to maximize profits, rather than social relations, and views leaders as exceptional individuals who heroically overcome the social context, rather than being dependent on it.

What is more often debated these days is the question to what extent leadership depends on social context. Is it a mere necessity for leadership qualities to correspond with the situational context? Or is it also the extent to which leadership is defined by the leader themselves, on one hand, and by the social context —followers — on the other? Constructionists find that leaders and followers are connected by nothing but a collectively constructed social identity (Reicher, Haslam & Hopkins 2005). While the constructivist school clearly finds that followers participate in the process of defining the leadership reality, it differs in the emphasis on follower importance. On one hand, there

---

13   Source: CESES 2007.

are scholars who, following Ervin Goffman's concept of impression management, define leadership as a social process where the leader changes the ways followers view him/her as well as themselves (Lord & Brown 2001), and thus consider the dominant leader role in defining shared identity as a condition of leadership. On the other hand, some find leadership primarily constructed by followers, rather than leaders. For example, James Meindl in his influential concept, "the romance of leadership", assumes that leader-follower relations are derived from followers constructions (Meindl 1995: 30).

Some constructionists avoid the question of follower importance in the construction of leadership or suggest that leaders and followers are equally important. We deduce this from the frequent opinion that there is a dialogue, rather than monologue, between leaders and followers, in which both parties act as partners. The topic of leader-follower dialogue is currently being developed by social identity scholars (Hogg 2001; Reicher, Haslam & Hopkins 2005). These scholars hold that one best becomes a leader by adapting to the ideal notion — or prototype — of leadership as provided by the collectively constructed social identity of leaders and followers.

The relational approach also assumes constant negotiation of the nature of leadership (style, authenticity, extent) between leaders and followers (Sinclair 2008: 84). From this perspective, a leader's success greatly depends on how his/her qualities and leadership styles are perceived by followers and whether these correspond to existing stereotypes about a suitable leadership style. Edwin Hollander considers followers an "attentive strategic audience" that gives credit to the leader if he/she has earned it through good leadership behavior. Leadership credit may grow or decline in time depending on the level of correspondence between how the leader is perceived to behave and an ideal/prototypical leadership behavior (Hollander 1993: 31–3). A leader's success, credit, and authenticity thus depend on the social context in which he/she acts, and more specifically, on the extent to which he/she embodies the predominant leadership ideal (prototype) in a given country, community, or organization.

1.2.1 Preferences and evaluations of leadership styles

We understand leadership style as how a leader leads followers to formulate and realize a shared vision, treats them, and applies his/her leadership capital in a given situation. Most studies of leadership styles construct ideal-typical leadership scales as a framework for interpreting leader behavior. Any given leader is usually expected to apply more than one leadership style. Most good leaders combine styles depending on the situation and their followers' preparedness.

A lesser leader usually retains one single style. We assume that leadership style choice is strongly influenced by the leader's values and qualities, as well as context, i.e. followers, other competing or cooperating leaders, or a broader social context. This begs the question, what basic types of leadership style are applied by Czech elites and how does this correspond to the expectations and preferences of the general public? Given the limited empirical data, we will reduce the choice of leadership styles under investigation to two dichotomies: (1) the autocratic versus democratic styles and (2) the transforming versus transactional styles. The autocratic and democratic styles, as parts of the basic leadership style repertoire, were identified by Kurt Lewin (1935) through a series of late 1930s experiments on modes of decision making.[14] The leader who takes the autocratic (authoritative) leadership style makes decisions without consulting others. The autocratic style tends to be effective whenever decision-making time is short and people's motivations to take part in follow-up activities do not depend on their involvement in the decision-making process. The democratic (participative) leadership style means that the leader involves people in decision-making, even if the decision-making process may be different from the leader's final decision, depending on the extent of negotiation with the group. While the leader makes the final decision, he/she encourages followers to participate. James McGregor Burns came up with the idea to juxtapose the transforming versus the transactional leadership styles. Transforming leadership not only assumes that people follow the leader who inspires them through his/her vision and passion for it but, moreover, leaders can be inspired by their followers. Both leaders and followers are able to "raise one another to higher levels of motivation and morality" (Burns 1978: 20). In contrast, a transactional leader offers a mere business deal to followers. Followers will receive rewards if they fulfill their leader's orders and wishes, and will be punished if they fail to do so.

---

14 Lewin also identified a third, highly participative leadership style, the so-called laissez-faire style. Here the leader is little involved in decision-making, people decide and take responsibility for their decisions and the leader is there mostly to encourage, coordinate, and show the aims of collective action. This style is often associated with situations where leaders are absent, rather than seen as part of the leadership style repertoire.

The autocratic versus democratic leadership styles

The "great man theory" implies that all important social events are the result of the strong willpower of some excellent personality that is capable of superhuman performance. According to this theory, every society must have its great heroes, its history makers, or else it would be without history. Time periods without a great man on stage are history-free periods. Despite its strong elitist character, this theory continues to be influential in the thinking of people in today's democratic societies. Thomas Carlyle, the author of the great man theory, suggested that every society has its characteristic hero repertoire that specifically shapes its history. Ladislav Holý developed a similar idea in his text on Czech national identity by stating that Czechs, in contrast to other nations, have many martyrs and very few hero-fighters in their national pantheon of great men. Based on two public opinion surveys of 1968 and 1992, the nation's top ten favorite or admired personalities included T. G. Masaryk, Jan Hus, Charles IV, and Jan Ámos Komenský. None of these nor any other top ten personality Czechs are proud of[15] is found to symbolize a hero-fighter by Holý (2001: 120–1). This indicates that Czechs reproduce a "peaceful nation" self-stereotype. In 2005, the Czech TV public modelled the BBC show "100 Greatest Britons". The top ten Czech personalities elected by about one hundred thousand respondents included the same four people mentioned above and just one hero-fighter, Jan Žižka (cf. Největší Čech 2005). The survey confirmed that Czech public opinion about the nation's history makers is rather stable and predominantly oriented towards peaceful personalities. None of the top admired personalities[16] may be considered a dictator or an autocratic personality. This strongly contrasts with the identified "mass hunger" for a great authoritarian man — a strong leader — in the Czech general public. Half of the respondents (48%) would prefer it if a strong political leader took power in order to put an end to squabbles in Parliament and to establish order.[17] Respondent views of an ideal society and elite morality suggest that such a leader should be a cold-blooded, non-corrupt technocrat (expert) rather than a warm-blooded and authoritarian visionary.

15 The 1992 top ten also included E. Beneš, L. Svoboda, J. Masaryk, M. R. Štefánik, and A. Dubček.
16 The Czech TV survey top ten also included Václav Havel, Jan Werich, Antonín Dvořák, Josef Čapek, and Božena Němcová.
17 Source: CESES 2008.

In order to explain the mass call for a strong leader, we must take a look at the Czech Republic's current situation. Is this situation absolutely normal, and does people's hunger for a strong leader derive from a general subconscious desire to submit to a stronger person, as described by Le Bon? Or is the Czech situation specific, are Czechs trying to avoid self-criticism about their role in modern history by projecting their best national traditions onto a strong leader? (Holý 2001: 148) Or is the Czech general public, facing the great themes of our time, trying to boost its self-confidence in order to better address those themes, as Tarde or Freud might find? Is the situation critical enough to induce fears in the general public, calling for a Weberian leader-savior, who emerges from the margins of society in times of crisis? Or is the situation characterized by strong public dissatisfaction with elite moral decay, which brings to life the Machiavellian archetype of a strong leader who, relying on popular support, protects the people from elites' oppressive and criminal practices? While all these explanations may partially apply to the current situation, the principal question, in our opinion, is: Is the Czech general public looking for the nation's savior, or rather an ally in its fight against elites? We find the latter options more plausible, as suggested by the above-mentioned public emphasis on the moral dimension of elite leadership, the strong criticism of elites for their unethical conduct, and little reflected crisis of prospective thinking (as exemplified by the effort to level off with the West's past). As if the general public were saying it would accept an authoritarian leader who would vigorously pursue public interest with regard to the vision of an efficient and socially just industrial society. Irresponsible elites are causing irregularities and chaos in social life, thus preventing the country from becoming a functioning model of an industrial society. And the general public is instinctively seeking a great man as an ally against the elites. The general public wants a morally strong leader, rather than an autocrat or a radical visionary. A leader is wanted who will win respect and impose order through the strength of his charisma.

The transforming versus transactional leadership styles

Burns holds that a transforming leader allows followers to fully realize their potential and creates a facilitative climate. He cooperates with followers to unveil latent needs. His role comprises of "helping to move followers up through the levels of need and the stages of moral development" (Burns 1978: 428). The leader himself must believe in his moral right to disturb followers from their tranquility and move them in a certain direction. "The leader's fundamental act is to induce people to be aware or conscious of what they feel — to feel their true needs so strongly, to define their values so meaningfully, that they can be moved to purposeful action." (Burns 1978: 43–44) In contrast, in the transactional leadership model, the leader-follower relationship is nothing but a particularized reciprocity, a give-and-take exchange based on momentary subjective desire. Burns considers transactional leadership an extremely conservative leadership type that prefers the status quo and prevents society from achieving desirable social change. In contrast, a transforming leader is able to assert radical change (within the framework of moral development). Burns emphasizes that transforming leadership brings much more utility to society than transactional leadership (Burns 1978). He argues that transforming leadership facilitates the mutual enrichment of leaders and followers that benefits all. This is impossible under transactional leadership, which is based on a mere reciprocity between particular egoisms. Similar ideas exist within the leader-member exchange theory (LMX) in that quality of leader-follower relations depends on mutual trust and respect. Leader-follower relations are poor when reduced to the mere fulfillment of formal commitments (Uhl-Bien, Graen & Scandura 2000). If the transformation of masses into a public is one of the principal elite agendas of our time, this means that elites should learn and apply the transforming leadership style.

This begs the question, are the Czech elites as society leaders actually leading their followers to higher levels of morality? Do they represent moral models? Do they respect follower interests and strive to enhance/emancipate them? Or are they rather buying up bottom-up support in order to keep their positions for as long as possible? The latter is the way half of the general adult population sees the Czech elites' leadership style. Only 10% agree with the opinion that the Czech elites use the transforming leadership style.[18] However, almost half of elite members do not share the predominant public opinion, and instead find their leadership style to be transforming. Less than one-fifth of elites identify with the transactional leadership style.

---

18 The transforming and transactional leadership styles were operationalized as a statement battery (questions 28a, 28b, 28c, 28d, 28f) about leader behavior. A new variable was constructed as a scale of preferences for the transforming leadership style, on one margin, and the transactional one, on the other margin. This variable (TRANSFOR) is an unweighted sum of the five responses, each on a five-point scale, making up a twenty-five-point scale. This was further transformed into a five-point scale (TRANSFO5). See Technical Appendix for details. Sources: CESES 2007 and 2008.

Table 1.9: What leadership styles the Czech elites use?

N = 2353/1037, percentages	General public	Elites
Strongly transforming	1	6
Rather transforming	9	41
Neutral	41	39
Rather transactional	38	14
Strongly transactional	11	1
Total	100	100

Sources: CESES 2007 and 2008.

Characteristically, elites tend to find the general public responsible for the currently poor elite-public relationship. They accuse the general public of violating the rules or of an opportunistic approach to the rules in place (67%). By doing so, they only confirm their own inability to lead the general public in the right direction. Leadership theory offers only two possible explanations for a situation when the general public violates the rules. Either the public is not following the elites or it is following their bad example. In both cases, elites are failing in leading the public. If elites are corrupt, the general public cannot be expected to act differently. Even most citizens themselves (68%) admit that people in the Czech Republic abide by the laws only when they find it personally favorable.[19]

It seems that we are witnessing the continuation of a special type of transactional leadership stemming from communist times. Then, elites were also corrupt and this was also tolerated by the general public. It was a give-and-take deal. Elites and the general public had a silent agreement which, from the elite perspective, went as follows: "You will let us rule and we will let you steal from the state." Today's law enforcement problems in the Czech Republic suggest that this silent agreement has been indeed extended. By admitting their opportunistic approach to laws, the general public is giving the following message to its elites: "You have nothing to blame us for because we are like you." At the same time, public discontent with elites suggests that the deal is not working out. Almost everyone could steal from the state during communist times, but this is impossible under the new democratic/market economy regime. Violating the laws brings little to the ordinary person, especially compared to how much

---

19   Sources: CESES 2007 and 2008.

this brings to elites. There were no such grave differences between elites and the general public under communism. Even these days, a relatively large group of people are able to live parasitically off of privatization and public procurement, but this is not enough. Elites cannot corrupt the general public in the way this was possible under the old regime because too many people are excluded from these opportunities.

1.2.2 Elite reputation and leadership

Authenticity

A dysfunctional market in visions undermines Czech elites' ability to lead the society whose institutions it is managing. Our data reveal that the general public tends to find ability to lead an attribute of elite status. The overwhelming majority of citizen respondents believe that only elites with leadership abilities may deserve the reputation of genuine/authentic elites. This can be derived from the fact that up to 79% of respondents find the "ability to lead people" an important or very important condition for someone to be considered an elite member. Moral/responsible behavior of people in leading positions is an equally important elite status characteristic. The ethical dimension of the leadership role, as suggested by, for instance, the Burns transforming leadership theory, is demanded by the public, and elites feel this as one of the most important commitments linked to their elite positions. Most elites (71%) feel the commitment to balance out their privileges through responsible behavior. We may conclude that, in this respect, elites agree with public opinion, at least verbally.[20]

Indeed, the Czech general public strongly associate authentic elite status with moral integrity. A factor analysis of the ways people evaluated the different elite status characteristics has revealed three factors behind their answers. As the strongest factor, the personal integrity factor includes leadership, moral qualities, and professional qualities. Authentic elites, as opposed to the real corrupt elites, should be fair, honest, and role models for everyone. At the same time, as opposed to the communist nomenclature elites of the past, they should be highly qualified and competent at leading society. In short, the general public ascribes the highest importance to those elite status characteristics Czech elites have been rather missing in recent history. Elite and leader authenticity is

---

20   Source: CESES 2007.

seen from the relational perspective. Citizens associate the authenticity of elite status and leadership with socially desirable behavior. Elite authenticity is not a neutral concept for them. One who acts according to his persuasion and for the benefit of others — followers — deserves the reputation of an authentic leader in the eyes of the Czech general public. Not only should the leader be "true to himself" under all circumstances, but he should also have a positive relationship with the community he is part of. Leaders should feel moral obligations to their followers or, more broadly, other people. The problem is that most citizens do not observe this in their elites.

Table 1.10: Factor analysis results for the question, "Are the following characteristics important for someone to be considered by you as an elite member?"

Rotated Component Matrix			
Total variance explained = 66.2%	**Factor**		
Public opinion N = 2300	**1. Integrity** 24.7% of variance	**2. Power** 23.2% of variance	**3. Distance** 18.3% of variance
Be a model for others	.629		
Higher education and qualifications	.848		
Fairness and honesty	.632		
Ability to lead people	.485		.504
Have many influential acquaintances		.826	
Hold an important top management function		.783	
Wealth		.774	
Popular attitude			.799
Popularity among people			.796

* Extraction Method: Principal Component Analysis. Rotation Method: Varimax with Kaiser Normalization, Rotation converged in 5 iterations.
Sources: CESES 2005.

The factor of power influences public thinking about the reputation of authentic elites only a little less importantly than personal integrity. Power is usually found to be an important leadership attribute. A powerless leader is normally deemed unable to lead followers and coordinate collective action. A leader must have power to both unleash and tame the emotions of followers, make them accept his/her vision, and get them to cooperate towards realizing the vision. A leader who loses power over his/her followers is no more in the lead. In our case, the power dimension is represented in the eyes of the general public by a circle of influential acquaintances, holding an important function, and wealth. Interestingly, Czechs tend to perceive elite power more strongly as a position in informal social networks, relative to wealth. Influential acquaintances appear to be an important part of elite status to three-fifths (59%) of respondents, while wealth appears so to only two-fifths (43%). This is also because an ordinary citizen's past experience with the role of informal social networks in the communist society clearly indicates that nothing can be achieved without good acquaintances and they are the key to wealth. At first sight, contemporary Czech elites might appear to have no problems fulfilling this status attribute: as many as three-fourths (77%) of citizen respondents believe that corrupt politicians, officials, and business people form a single interconnected network.[21] Given the fact that an overwhelming majority of the general public condemns elite corruption and clientelism and demands that they act responsibly, these kinds of informal networks cannot be expected to be considered part of an authentic elite leadership within society. An ordinary citizen simply believes that influential acquaintances are not necessarily clientelist, and instead, belong to genuine elites because they facilitate their actions for the public good.

The social distance factor also proves to be relatively strong in people's perceptions of elite leadership reputation. There are two basic approaches to the social distance between leaders and followers. On one hand, the elitist approach raises leaders high above their followers, endowing them with such great qualities and deeds an ordinary follower cannot even think of. On the other hand, the plebeian view of leadership sees a potential leader in every person and accepts the view that practically everyone can become a leader if they are in the right place at the right time. The elitist approach assumes a hierarchic leader-follower relationship. The leader is supreme and the followers look up to him. The best of the best become elitist leaders and ideals are high on their agenda. A plebeian leader is only "the first among equals". He primarily serves his followers. Social distance is seen as one of the key factors in leader reputation and legitimacy. (Antonakis & Atwater 2002) Data analysis reveals that the Czech general public clearly prefers the plebeian reputation in their leaders and expects authentic elites to have a popular attitude (66%) and be popular (79%).

---

21   Source: CESES 2008.

The predominant preference of a small leader-follower social distance is hardly surprising in a democratic society. Similarly, modern leaders normally put on display their proximity to followers. The latter has often been reduced to a mere cliché — leaders acting as plebeians. Leaders want a human face — and often a popular face — in order to get their followers to like, trust, and continue to support them. However, as we will explain below, the plebeian leaning is on a decline among Czech elites. The question of what level of leader-follower social distance/proximity is possible and practical for effective leadership remains open? On one hand, the elitist distance from followers is seen as a condition for maintaining respect and enhancing leader control over followers.[22] If a leader is too close to his followers, he risks losing authority and becoming one of them. On the other hand, if he is too far away, he risks being torn from followers and losing their trust. This leadership dilemma is indicated in the Czech public attitudes by the fact that, on one hand, the public desires a strong leader whose authority would rise above others, and on the other hand, they do not want the leader's authority to get out of public control.

The quality of leaders

We can study the effectiveness of how elites fulfill their leadership roles by verifying if their visions have been fulfilled. To what extent these visions have become reality is, however, less important for leadership ratings than the ways citizens perceive this. Do most citizens perceive that leaders' visions and promises have become reality under the current situation? However, there is more than just the discrepancy between promises and reality. Such a discrepancy can be a positive thing for many, after all. According to Keith Dowding, the quality of leaders is most importantly rated by two factors: (1) how opinion differences between leaders and the general population are overcome; and (2) how people evaluate the change brought through vision implementation. If someone wants to be seen as a strong or great leader, they not only have to do the right things, but also have to do the right things in spite of predominant public opinion (Dowding 2008: 4). A leader deserves a greater reputation in the eyes of the public if he/she has had to overcome major doubts about his/her vision and if the general public finds the vision implementation

---

22 Some authors (Hofstede 1980; Gabriel 1997; Collinson 2005) consider it generally accepted that leader distance and power are mutually supportive: "...distance can perpetuate power and power can perpetuate distance" (Collinson 2005: 245).

to have brought about a greater common good. If the leader manages to implement his vision in spite of the fact that it was contrary to the opinion of most of the population, and if most of the population ultimately acknowledges that it brought about a change to the better, then he/she will certainly win a great man's reputation. The leader has been able to mobilize followers under unfavorable circumstances and realize change that proved to be good.

If most people find the change brought through vision implementation positive, but if the leader has not had to overcome opinion differences, he deserves only a mediocre reputation in the public's eyes. He is a leader who goes with the flow, and luckily in the right direction. If the leader's vision corresponds with majority opinion but its implementation has, in majority opinion, not brought the promised positive change, he gets a weak leader's reputation. He is a leader who goes with the flow but, unfortunately, in the wrong direction. And finally, a leader whose vision contradicted majority public opinion and most people believe that its realization has caused a change for the worse gets a catastrophic leader reputation. He is a leader who not only goes against the flow but moreover in the wrong direction. This leader reputation typology is based on the dual criteria of opinion differences and change evaluations, as a loose paraphrase of Dowding's leader authority concept, and is presented in the following table.

Table 1.11: A leader reputation typology

	Vision was initially **in line** with majority public opinion	Vision initially **contradicted** majority public opinion
Vision implementation is perceived by most people as **positive** change	Mediocre leader	Great/strong leader
Vision implementation is perceived by most people as **negative** change	Weak leader	Catastrophic leader

Source: Adapted from Dowding (2008: 4).

Now we can ask the question, what is the leadership reputation of Czech elites? Some answers have been given by public opinions about their authenticity, morality, and leadership qualities. However, the quality of current Czech elites' leadership is not easy to assess, not only because usually no one stands by failed visions. More importantly, it is difficult to tell which visions, which leaders, and which time period should be chosen as representative. Here we will utilize Wasilewski's three-stage developmental model of post-communist societies, which makes it possible to reduce the repertoire of visions and assign specific visions to the different post-communist development stages. The transition stage is, in this model, associated with the vision of perfecting the regime change. It is symbolized in the Czech Republic by two men, Václav Havel and Václav Klaus, who pursued rigorous democratization and the rapid adoption of capitalism without transitory periods. These visions indeed initially contradicted the opinion of most people, who desired a kind of enhanced socialism, rather than liberal democracy and full-blown capitalism.[23] Havel and Klaus became great leaders in the eyes of the general public because they had to fight to assert their visions against majority opinion and, eventually, received positive ratings for regime change. Even today, most of the general public (65%) and elites (94%) believe that the 1989 regime change was worth it. While a full generalization is impossible, the transition stage in the Czech society clearly generated some great leaders. Their grandiose reputation shone upon the rest of the country's transition elites, who had sided with their vision of dissociation from socialism.

The heroic times of transition quickly passed and new, more specific visions of functioning democracy and economic reforms had to be offered for the new transformation stage. However, the transformation visions of Havel and Klaus were sharply contradictory from the very beginning. While Havel envisioned a democracy resting on a strong civic society and did not usually comment on the nature of economic reforms, Klaus vigorously asserted a vision of laissez-faire capitalism and a standard representative democracy, and was reserved towards civic society organizations. Initial public opinion was on Klaus's side but with growing economic problems grew the doubts of the general public about the benefits of the changes Klaus's reforms had brought about. With that, the leadership of Václav Klaus began to decline. Even worse, the general public began to view the voucher privatization, the magnet of his reforms, as a symbol of elite conspiracy against ordinary people.[24]

---

23 In a representative survey of December 1989, only 3 per cent of respondents favored the pursuit of a capitalist way of development. 41% wanted to continue on the way of socialism, and 52% chose a third way between capitalism and socialism (Slejška et al. 1990: 51).

24 In a 2008 representative survey by GfK Prague, the belief that coupon privatisation was a fraud scheme represented the most popular conspiracy theory in the Czech Republic. Two-thirds (65%) of respondents agreed that coupon privatization was intentionally planned in order to make a selected group of people rich (Frič 2008: 13).

However, Havel's leadership reputation within the Czech public suffered a great deal as well. Unable to implement his robust democratic vision in practice, he earned the image of a dreamer and impractical moralist, failing to mobilize followers and step up to the front line in order to lead the struggle to realize his visions.

Popular disaffection arose from the failure to fulfill Klaus's vision for the country to become a Central European economic tiger. This opened up space for left-wing leaders, amongst which Miloš Zeman, the chairman of the Czech Social Democratic Party, stood out. Zeman became famous through his defamatory statement equaling coupon privatization to "the fraud of the century". His vision of a "social market economy" was presented as sharply contrasting with Klaus's liberal market economic vision, yet in line with the predominant ideal of a well-functioning industrial society. However, few believed that such a vision could be accomplished through increased government spending. Zeman's take on assembly plants began to be implemented under his leadership. The "ruined country" he argued to have inherited from Klaus was transformed, under Zeman's leadership, into a prosperous open economy. Therefore, Zeman, now the country's Prime Minister, was perceived by the general public as a great leader in the beginning of the consolidation stage. This, however, did not last long because the changes his consolidating efforts brought about fell behind popular expectations. Today's economic crisis, which primarily hit the car industry, has put in question the value of the results brought about through the implementation of Zeman's vision. At the time he was leaving office, most of the general population clearly was not finding the consolidation stage agenda accomplished. This is documented by the following table indicating that, in the eyes of most of the general population and elites alike, the consolidation of Czech society is not accomplished to this date.

We find this fact, along with the broadly perceived absence of visions, crucial for assessing the quality of Czech elite leadership. No great leaders can exist when the Czech general public feels great visions are absent and the expected positive changes have not occurred. Furthermore, citizens desire a strong leader because they feel no one is able to convince the majority of his vision in order to benefit all. The Czech elites are perceived to have lost their ability to breed leaders who rigorously fight for the realization of great visions. In short, great leaders have mostly abandoned the Czech political stage as solutions to society's consolidation problems have come to long-term inertia.

Table 1.12: Are the following aspects characteristic for the Czech Republic after the years of post-1989 development?

General Public 2005, N = 2300; 2008, N = 2353; Elites 2007, N = 1037; percentages	Agree/Strongly agree		
	GP 2005	GP 2008	Elites 2007
a	Open and fair economic competition	18	31	49
b	Media have excessive power	64	66	65
c	Every citizen's rights and dignity are protected	24	39	61
d	Social prosperity through debt	75	82	87
e	Open and fair competition among political parties	17	20	32
f	High corruption within public administration	77	80	70

Sources: CESES 2005, 2007, and 2008.

1.2.3 Leadership culture

Further contextual factors behind the variability of elite leadership patterns include generally accepted cultural values pertaining to leader roles and leader-follower relations. Clearly, leader beliefs about their roles and relations with followers do not exist in a void. The given cultural context works as a set of limiting or stimulating factors in that certain leadership styles and ways of leadership capital accumulation/activation are preferred. Every society has its specific, deeply embedded cultural leadership values and beliefs and collective mentalities influencing leader and follower behavior that are part of their shared identity. We understand collective leader mentality as a set of shared value orientations reflecting the predominant collective identity of leaders and followers in a given society or community. We assume that neither leaders nor followers can abruptly and easily free themselves of the cultural behavioral patterns that have traditionally applied to their roles. The collective leader mentality is, therefore, a cultural model (tradition) of leadership behavior that is generally accepted in a given society. The collective leader mentality is a "supra-individual phenomenon" (Durkheim) that effectively pressures leaders to act in line with the existing model. We further assume the existence of a similar follower mentality. The leadership and followership mentalities find themselves in mutual interaction, which makes them converge. The mentalities of successful leaders and their followers will be similar. We will study the traditional Czech model of collective leader mentality in two of its dimensions that, in our opinion, best reflect the specific nature of Czech elites' collective leader mentality. Each dimension is defined through two poles. They are (1) the elitist versus plebeian mentalities and (2) the European versus provincial mentalities. In our opinion, the nature of these mentalities, as cultural context factors, gives us the answer to the following important question about the elite-public relationship in the Czech Republic: "Why does the Czech general public tolerate non-authentic and amoral leaders?"

The aristocratic versus the plebeian mentalities

This dimension of the cultural context of Czech elite leadership behavior reflects an important and oft-debated aspect of the Czech leader mentality that was inherited from the lengthy time periods with absence of Czech national (aristocratic) elites, including the period of communist rule. It is related to the problem of the Czech elites' historic discontinuity (cf. Pehe 1998, Svátek 1993) that dates back to the first half of the 17th century when, after the 1620 Battle of White Mountain, Bohemia and Moravia lost their nobility. The nobility never fully recovered and never became the leading force in society. Its positions were taken by either foreign aristocracy members (frowned upon by the local population) or domestic elites of plebeian origin (underestimated and laughed at by the population). Throughout the past hundred years, different Czech elites repeatedly came to power but only for short periods of time, during which they did not manage to create a new tradition of Czech elite rule and overcome their own plebeian complex. During communist rule, leader elitism was frowned upon, and instead, plebeian qualities were highly valued in leaders. This caused a plebeian syndrome in Czech elites — the fact that elitism is not in their blood even if they hold leading positions in the society. Contemporary Czech elites are in a similar situation, constantly balancing the commitments of their dual —aristocratic and plebeian — mentalities. Therefore, let us clarify the respective meanings of the two mentalities.

The *aristocratic mentality* is often described as elitism, part of the collective mentality of the ruling group of people who consider themselves the only natural elite, "the best of the best". Elitism is associated with individualist emphases (in lifestyle, work, sports, etc.) and efforts to stand out and distinguish self from others. Emphases on style, fine taste, affectation, sophistication, and fine manners belong to the aristocratic mentality. Conservatism, which finds social and power inequalities part of the natural order, dominates its views of society: a minority must always rule and is entitled to privileges. No real alternative to the current situation is accepted, since the situation is the best of all possible ones. Typical is a deep-rooted belief in the legitimacy of one's own privileged position, along with a strong sense of duty to society and voluntary self-restraint (Ortega y Gasset). Out of the belief in one's own exceptional qualities grows the feeling of natural superiority over the population, the vulgar mass, the rabble, which must be kept at an appropriate distance. No public exists, there are only masses, and those cannot decide on public affairs because they are incompetent. Elites, rather than masses (or, in the best case, the people) protect democratic values, because the latter are passive and tend to fall for demagogues. The aristocratic mentality embraces strong resistance to the collective civic activism, organized protest,[25] and of course any "counter-elites" possibly arising from such activism. The pursuit of elitism also requires elites to maintain consensus (Burton, Gunther, Higley 1992), i.e. stick together, enhance internal elite solidarity and integrity, and thus help everyone stay in their elite positions.

The *plebeian mentality* is one of the ordinary people who despise everything sophisticated and follow simplicity and pragmatism. It embraces collectivism, mass consumption, mass entertainment, and collective sports. It is characteristic for its efforts to be in line with others, avoid standing out, hide through mimicry, and avoid causing envy. Such efforts may grow into fearful opportunism, one that commands keeping a low profile and staying out of trouble. People of the plebeian mentality tend to rely on the government paternalistically, demand their rights but forget about their duties. They want to enjoy life now, without unnecessary self-denial and thinking about the distant future. In the Czech context, they are characterized through a "traditional hedonistic model of food and chatter in a peaceful beer high" (Machačová and Matějček 2002: 459). The plebeian mentality is egalitarian, dislikes social inequalities and formal hierarchies. It emphasizes popular wisdom and ordinary people's merits in protecting democracy from predatory elites. Elites should only do what people desire: "the people's voice is the voice of God." The "mental plebeian" (Pehe 1998) holds contempt for elites because money can buy membership to the elite club. An aristocrat is in his eyes no better than an ordinary person. The plebeian mentality is constantly suspicious of elite conspiracy against the people. Elites are responsible for all evil in the society, and they are good as scapegoats in

---

25 NGOs are supposed to collect rubbish in the park, remove cans from rivers, and avoid politics.

bad times. The plebeian mentality also embraces radicalism, rebellion, anti-elitism, and a lack of respect for authorities. On the other hand, it is also associated with the cult of great leaders, especially those of plebeian origin, who had to go through the martyrdom of prisons, prosecutions, emigration, etc. (Michels) and thus have redeemed their leader privileges. In their relations wiht other plebeians, people of the plebeian mentality are envious. They do not want one of them to work their way up to an elite position. No one plebeian is good enough to become part of the elite. Therefore, they try to drag everyone down, thwart their plans to step up, and "mud everyone who stands out above the average in any way" (Pehe 1998).

The aristocratic and plebeian mentalities are parts of the Czech cultural context which, to a great extent, influences the effectiveness of Czech elite leadership. Some elite members refer to those mentalities when trying to explain why the Czech elites actually do not lead or why Czechs are unable to rule themselves. Two general hypotheses are most often mentioned. According to the first hypothesis, the plebeian mentality is difficult to manage because of its strong egalitarianism, quarreling, and lack of respect for leader authority (cf. Pehe 1998). Czech classic František Palacký identified this defect of the national character as a "sign of our perpetual political immaturity" (Palacký 1912: 17). This hypothesis ultimately means that Czechs are bad followers. According to the second hypothesis, elites basically cannot lead society because they are plebeian, and therefore, do not constitute genuine elites with leadership in their blood. As mentioned above, only a minority of Czech elite members spontaneously admits to or consciously agrees with the fact that being a member of the elite means more than just behave oneself — leading others and being aware of their mission is one of the elite duties that may require bringing sacrifices. Where the absence of leadership in responses by elite members goes beyond a merely spontaneous, unconscious reaction and becomes an elaborate attitude, we may find Czech elites rebel against being considered natural elites, "the best of the best". Throughout the 1990s, there were abundant examples of elite members denying being any better than other people, in other words, emphasizing their plebeian nature.[26] After all, this was just a continuation of the "plebeian nation" tradition that rooted deep during the 1920s and 1930s and was strongly reinforced during communism. Elite members are ambivalent about themselves

---

26   E.g. Husák 1997.

in refusing the accusations of being no genuine, natural leaders of the society, on one hand, and rebelling against being expected to be better than others, to have exceptional leadership qualities on the other hand. The above findings support the media-generated idea that the Czech elites in fact do not aspire to lead society anywhere. They rather prefer being influenced by and following public opinion because they usually do not have any vision of their own or are afraid of publicizing it (thus assuming responsibility for it). Therefore, from the leader/follower mentality perspective, Czechs cannot rule themselves because they are both bad leaders and bad followers.

However, elite opinions do not confirm hypothesis no. 2 that elites cannot lead society because of their plebeian nature. Most elite respondents lean to the elitist worldview, rather than the plebeian one.[27] This is most marked in economic elites. The times when maintaining an image of minimum social distance from common people was part of "good manners" are long gone. The Czech elites are not ashamed of their elite positions and mostly do not find it necessary to demonstrate a plebeian unity with the lower social strata. This is most pronounced in the media elites (54% of which identify with elitism). Civic elites most often reject elitism (13%). On the other hand, hypothesis no. 1 about the plebeian nature of the Czech general population (non-elites) has been mostly confirmed. More than one-fourth (27%) of the general adult population show a plebeian mentality and half have at least some plebeian elements in their character.[28] The plebeian tendency is clearly not as strong as the hypothesis might suggest. Most citizens are not radically plebeian. They are nominally plebeian, i.e. by their origin, rather than mentality.

As we have seen, while the Czech elites have mostly overcome their plebeian syndrome, doubts about their leadership qualities continue to exist, even in their own ranks. Those doubts are a result of current elites' practical behavior. The Czech elites are far from seeking the "heroic lives" of aristocrats, as Malleuish (2006) would expect. They are rather "flying low" and, if possible, trying not to stand out. Expressions of plebeian

---

27　The elitist and plebeian mentalities were operationalized as four statements (questions 4f, 27c, 46d, and 46e) indicating attitudes to the relationship between society and the individual. A new auxiliary variable was constructed as a scale between plebeianism and elitism. This variable (NARIST17) is an unweighted sum of the four responses. It was further transformed into a five-point scale (NARIST05) equal to the scale of response options for the questions it comprises of. See Technical Appendix for details.

28　Sources: CESES 2007 and 2008.

anti-elitism by elite members themselves are not unusual.[29] Furthermore, the authenticity problem is also associated with the elite-plebeian question in the Czech Republic. Given the historic discontinuity of the Czech elites, every leader who wants to be authentic has to juggle being an elite member and simultaneously not losing links with the stratum he came from, which represents the background of his authenticity. Since almost all members of the contemporary elites have been recruited from people of "low descent", they have to stop being themselves (i.e. plebeians) in order to become part of the nation's natural elite. In conclusion, elites verbally solve this dilemma in favor of elitism but, in the eyes of the general public, their real behavior greatly lags behind the aristocratic model.

Table 1.13: Elites and the general public on a scale between the elitist and the plebeian mentalities

N = 2353/1037, percentages	General public	Elites
Strongly elitist	2	5
Rather elitist	13	40
Medium	59	49
Rather plebeian	23	6
Strongly plebeian	4	1
Total	100	100

Sources: CESES 2007 and 2008.

The European versus the provincial mentalities

The problem of the Czech elites' historic discontinuity implies that modern Czech society had to be built bottom-up. Since its birth in the 19th century, it has been primarily a society of farmers and small-town bourgeoisie, with an almost complete absence of elites above the local and regional levels. In this small, provincial environment, one could hardly expect a great personality to be born whose perspective would go beyond the Czech Lands of the then Habsburg monarchy.

---

29 This is exemplified by the following words of President Klaus: "We have to be with the ordinary people, rather than with elites. Elites do not want freedom for all, they want freedom and exceptional positions for themselves. They do not seek market rewards for their work. Elites have been more dangerous foes of the Czech way out of the Hayekian communist slavery than the defeated communists and their friends." (Klaus 2005)

It was a society whose unity went beyond language and where vertical differences were frowned upon. As Jan Patočka wrote in his famous essay about Czechs, "higher strata practically did not exist and had to be created. In that process, the goal was to maintain close contact between all parts of society, rather than create steep social differentiation." (Patočka 1992: 12) Instead of seeking sufficient distance in order to acquire the perspective necessary for knowledge within a broader context, conditions were conducive for getting absorbed in internal national issues and domestic squabble. Such an environment "is not conducive for raising leading men" (Patočka 1992: 12). Those only arise rarely and somewhat randomly, as exemplified by T. G. Masaryk. He, however, did not break out of isolation and create offspring, according to Patočka. Patočka's description of the Czech national situation corresponds to what can be named as Czech provincialism as induced by historic circumstances. Jiří Pehe also blames history for Czechs' provincial self-centeredness and escape into their own micro-world. He maintains that Czech provincialism is hardly surprising given that the Czech Lands were for centuries a province of Austria-Hungary, later a Third Reich protectorate, and even later a periphery of the Soviet empire. For centuries, decisions about Czechs were not made in Prague, and therefore, it was only natural that Czechs reserved the mundane nature for those in charge (Pehe 1996). However, this statement is not quite precise. Czechs' mental restraint in their "little history"[30] did not emerge at once and was not total. Modern Czech social history can be understood, according to Patočka, as the nation's tragic struggle to break free from the confinement of its little history, one that has never been won, even when victory was close (Patočka 1992: 14–15).

We can only add one thing: the struggle between provincial and mundane tendencies did not end with the fall of the communist regime, and continues today. It has been particularly visible in the ongoing public debate about the Czech role in the European Union. As mentioned above, the westernization of Czech society has been restrained by the closed-up mentality and provincial self-centeredness of the elites and general population alike. As a strategy for our actions within the EU, both elites and the general public most often support defending the sovereignty of the Czech Republic. These facts have posed urgent challenges for leadership in Czech elites and greatly shaped the social

---

30 "The little Czech history has been a struggle of this bottom-up society for growth and equality." (Patočka 1992: 11)

context they have to adapt to, in one way or another. Let us take a look at the current position of Czechs on the scale between the provincial and the European mentalities. Data collected demonstrate that the European mentality is more often represented in elites, with the economic elite segment being the most supportive. In contrast, the political elites are the least European, and are rather closer to the provincial mentality of the general public.

Table 1.14: Leader mentality

N = 1037, percentages	European	Medium	Provincial	Total
Plebeian	1	3	3	7
Medium	17	19	12	48
Elitist	19	17	9	45
Total	37	39	24	100

Source: CESES 2007.

In spite of general expectations, the Czech elites lean to elitism and the European mentality, rather than the plebeian mentality and provincialism. This strongly differentiates them from the general public, which is rather plebeian and provincial—but not as strongly as it might seem from the mass proliferation of tabloid newspapers or some circumstances of Czech historical development. Nevertheless, the contradiction between the generally shared image and actual reality is greater than in elites. It is certainly interesting to know what proportion of elites behaving in plebeian and provincial ways is enough for the elite as a whole to be viewed as plebeian/provincial by commentators and critics. Even more interesting would be to find out what proportion of elites would have to behave in aristocratic and mundane ways so that elites lose their plebeian/provincial label. Unfortunately, we do not have a time series in order to find out trends in the Czech elites' image and actual mentality. Of course, there is the above-mentioned difference between the elite and the public mentalities, which is also rather generally unknown. Elites are clearly ahead of the general public in terms of levelling off with the West, but they probably are not communicating this sufficiently. They are not trying to behave as apparent transforming leaders who raise their followers' thinking and behavior to the level of Western societies.

Table 1.15: Follower mentality

N = 2353, percentages	European	Medium	Provincial	Total
Plebeian	1	6	19	27
Medium	6	19	33	59
Elitist	4	5	6	15
Total	12	30	58	100

Source: CESES 2008.

One of the principal findings of our survey is that while the general public is critical of the current situation, most people do not tend to agree with radical solutions.[31] Therefore, the current elite-public relations seem to be stable. This begs the question, what kind of elite-public equilibrium has formed throughout the past twenty years? Is it a combination of plebeian elites and indifferent masses, as the Czech media sometimes portray it? Or does it comprise of aristocratic elites and an engaged civic public, a combination likely to be predominant in developed Western societies? Quite surprisingly, the data collected tend to speak in favor of the latter option. About one-third (32%) of the general adult population in the Czech Republic are active citizens and members in non-governmental organizations.[32] In contrast, only slightly above one-fourth (27%) of respondents are passive citizens. The remaining two-fifths (41%) are somewhere in between civic activism and passivity. Thus, elites with an aristocratic mentality and a not-quite-passive public indeed represent the most frequent combination. However, the situation is nothing to cheer. A critical citizen as an opinion leader or effective and courageous follower is far from predominant in the Czech Republic, and rather represents an endangered species that urgently needs a transforming leader's helping hand.

Conclusion

In conclusion, the elite-public divergence lies in the ways elite leadership qualities and moral integrity are rated. Most elites believe that they have

31 On the other hand, 26% of respondents (CESES 2008) more or less side with the opinion that the regime of our society should be changed radically, and in absolute terms, this is a scary number of people. This is particularly alarming given the fact that these people represent a potential waiting for a populist leader to turn it into a narrow-thinking, passionate crowd.

32 It is, however, not quite clear whether this part of the population represents Mills's true public or Habermas's civic public that is capable of public deliberation.

leadership qualities and are not corrupt. In contrast, most members of the general public find elites unable to lead as well as corrupt. As a result, the general public either does not follow elites or elites are not leading by example. The Czech general public is reserved to following Western models and demands that elites come up with an original, specifically Czech, modernization vision. In other words, elites are expected to assume a leadership role in society without relying on Western models. However, the Czech elites have been unable to offer a more detailed vision for the future most people would accept. For this they have deserved various defamatory labels and a great deal of mistrust from the general public. According to a large part of the Czech general public, our elites do not aspire for skilled and moral leadership in society, and instead, engage in secret cartel agreements, backstage manipulations, and corrupt collaboration. There is no decent vision for levelling off with the West. Therefore, while Czechs are not lagging behind in terms of technology, they seem to have missed their chance to develop prospective thinking (in elites and the public alike). They are falling behind in their priorities. They cannot level off with the West by modeling its past. So far, no one seems to particularly mind this. The crisis of the future remains little reflected.

The ordinary citizen tends to complain about his elites, in line with tradition. Otherwise, his behavior ranges from loyalty to resignation. He maintains his careful and comfortable life strategy of resting comfortably in the mainstream. On the other hand, elites are clearly satisfied with their easy role, getting by, merely pretending genuine leadership. They find levelling off with the West a nice goal that should not be wasted by being accomplished. Then they would have to work and come up with something else. It is easier this way for elites and the public alike. As mentioned above, success cannot occur where leaders and followers go easy on each other, only striving to survive comfortably without unnecessary difficulties in the contest for better positions. With such a pseudo-leadership and pseudo-followership, i.e. if Czechs only pretend that real change is desired, a less prosperous community or society will ensue in the long term.

The Czech elites do not consider their kind plebeian but are considered as such by the general public. Through its negative ratings of elite moral and leadership qualities, the public is sending the following message: "Do not play aristocrats because you are only one of us." Elites seen as plebeians cannot count on the mechanism of mass identification with an ideal worth following (Freud 1996: 88) because they do not embody such an ideal. Since they are no genuine, natural elites, they do not have the suggestive power of those charismatic leaders embodying a collective ideal. This situation seemingly has one advantage: elites are unable to fool the general public and turn it into a fanatical crowd. This, however, will only apply until a truly charismatic populist leader emerges who will be able to manipulate the public with the lure of anti-elitism. While the Czech elites pretend to be society's leaders, they are not very successful at it. They blame the low level of civic culture within the general public. In turn, the Czech general public likes seeing its elites fall to their knees in the plebeian dust, something many people experienced during communism and continue to experience today. No one seems good enough for elite leader positions, as if they wanted no elites at all (Kandert 2002). They dislike the growing distance between elites and ordinary citizens and are often nostalgic about the old communist times when "all were equal" and even political leaders were bound to demonstrate their plebeian nature.

Even if the Czech elites have mostly overcome their plebeian syndrome, a general crisis of prospective thinking suggests that Czechs continue to form the Patočkian "society of freed servants" not knowing what to do with themselves. Elites are not leading society and citizens are not following established rules. Elites are little demanding of the public and vice versa. Elites have little leadership capital but no one seems to find this problematic. The citizens complain about elites but mostly are not becoming radicalized. Elites get by, pretending leadership, and the general public, in turn, often excuses its wrongdoings by pointing to the bad elite example. Both sides are comfortable with this undemanding environment. To generalize Ortega y Gasset's words, neither side is addressing the "task of our time". Given the Czech public inclination for the industrial society vision, elite reluctance to assume the leadership role facilitates the construction of an industrial theme park in the Czech Republic, diverting both parties' attention from the levelling off with the Western (information) societies.

2. Cohesion and Sustainability of Democratic Elites

Pavol Frič and Martin Nekola

The perpetual dilemma of democratic elites

Elite theory scholars studying Central European post-communist countries have long been involved with the question of elite changes after the collapse of totalitarian regimes in the region. In the center of their attention stood the relationship between "old and new elites", i.e. the old regime "nomenclature elites" and the elites forming after the communist regimes collapsed. We believe that after twenty years of political and economic transformation, the question of elite changes/continuity during transformation has exhausted its explanatory potential. All Central European post-communist countries have finalized their institutional transformations. And as stated in Chapter 1 by Frič and Bednařík, the modernization process of "levelling off with the West" and the role of elites therein has been posed ever more often as the theme of our times. The situation has reversed radically in that democratic elites represent the "old elites" of today, struggling to retain their positions. Therefore, the issue of democratic elite continuity and long-term sustainability appears much more relevant today. The Czech elites have been in a specific situation, based on their historic trajectory characterized by repeated discontinuity and multiple changes of democratic and autocratic regimes within the past ninety years.[33] Moreover, the Czech society has repeatedly experienced elite failure during crisis situations in modern history, often referred to as "the fatal eights". In 1938, 1948, and 1968, the Czech elites faced external pressures on the integrity of their collective identities, and threats of losing the leadership roles they had assumed and used to legitimate their privileges in the Czech society before the respective

---

33 Cf. Pehe (1998) and Svátek (1993) for more on the historic discontinuity of Czech elites.

crises. They submitted to the pressures in all three cases, losing face vis-à-vis most members of the Czech general public. During extreme crisis situations, the Czech elites have usually acted in such ways that they lost public trust and support, i.e. the necessary tools to overcome crisis. In all three cases, they were unable to lead by moral example and get decisive parts of the general public on their side; unable to utilize any moral ethos of resistance within the society to confront the crisis both externally and internally. They were always the first to abandon ship, giving up their leadership roles. The desolate public became frustrated, chaos and panic prevailed. As a result, members of the general public retreated from the public space, seeking private and solitary survival strategies. Therefore, it seems justified to ask the question today, how long will democratic elites be able to control the growing extremism in the times of economic crisis and prevent a strong plebiscitary leader from taking power?

The reasons for the past failures of the Czech democratic elites have often been identified in their disunified character.[34] On the other hand, the communist regime experience has made it crystal clear that the existence of a small, cohesive elite is contrary to democracy. Therefore, how can we make sense of the relationship between the cohesion of democratic elites, their sustainability, and preserving democracy as such? What cohesion model and what structure of elite-public relations determine the sustainability of democratic elites? What should the relations between the different elite segments look like in order to guarantee a stable democracy: in order to prevent democracy from falling into tyranny or anarchy, prevent the hegemony of one single elite, and prevent the collapse of power structures and the subsequent loss of effective leadership in the society? Do we know at all where to find the desired balance between the principles of democracy and autocracy, as referred to by the elite theory classic, Gaetano Mosca (1939: 429)? In his eyes, ideal governance implied equilibrium between plebiscitary and bureaucratic elements. Generally speaking, elite theory throughout its history viewed the cohesion of democratic elites as both a threat and a condition for their sustainability. In short, democracy requires a certain balance in the principles regulating relations between the different elite segments. The goal is for elites to be cohesive, but not too much, and at the same time, incohesive, but again to a certain level. However, identifying and maintaining the right level of unity and differentiation is a very difficult task. At the same time, if elite theory is unable to solve

---

34 See the above example of three "fatal eights": 1938, 1948, and 1968.

the perpetual dilemma of democratic elites adequately, it will have little predictive ability and little practical relevance. Therefore, knowledge of the ideal equilibrium in intra-elite and elite-public relations in a stable democracy would be useful for ensuring the long-term prosperity of democratic societies. Who and in what ways guarantees that such an equilibrium continues to be identified and maintained? How can democratic elites avoid their own gradual transformation into a rigid power pyramid, on one hand, or an exceedingly horizontal and impotent structure, on the other hand? How should democratic elites balance wisely between the two poles of their perpetual dilemma? Over time, elite theory scholars have provided different answers to the perpetual democratic elite dilemma and have identified different ways of running the *perpetuum mobile democraticum*.

Elite cohesion and openness

Classic elitists assumed that finding permanent power equilibrium is an impossible task in every society. Democracy was seen as a particularly unstable governance project. Democracy would sooner or later fall into a masked oligarchy or an autocracy of demagogues. Such a transformation was, however, not dramatized and, instead, seen as inevitable and a matter of course. Therefore, little attention was paid to the ways of preventing it. More attention was devoted to the general problem of how an existing elite can sustain its positions; prevent losing its power in involuntary or even violent/revolutionary ways in favor of another emerging elite; and stay in power for as long as possible. Pareto was most concerned with solving this problem. In his concept of elite changes, he wrote about maintaining balance between "consolidators" and "innovators" within elites. Innovators (foxes and speculators) lead society to changes and attempt reforms in order to achieve greater prosperity. In contrast, consolidators (lions and rentiers) primarily struggle for social stability and defend the "good old times". Consolidators find themselves constantly fighting with innovators over leadership in society. Elite sustainability ideally requires balanced proportions of innovators and consolidators within society so that one group effectively controls any excess by the other group. However, this is not sustainable because the social situation is in constant development and requires solutions that can be provided by either consolidators or innovators. Weak innovators fail in situations requiring power solutions and are replaced by consolidators, who do not hesitate to use violent force but, at the same time, tend to close up in their own shells, slowing down "elite circulation" and making elites "degenerate".[35] In this situation, consolidators have two options: either they voluntarily give power back to innovators in order to speed up circulation, or they will be overthrown by an emerging counter-elite. However, Pareto believed that such a smooth elite circulation in the interest of ongoing revitalization is not permanently sustainable. Ruling elites are bound to lose their elite positions sooner or later (Pareto 1966: 131).

The isolation of the ruling elite — its fortification in privileged positions — was understood by Pareto as a result of elite moral failure, i.e. the greed and arrogance of elites in excluding others from the benefits of their own positions. Pareto identified two basic characteristics of decadent elites: (1) they become weak and humanitarian (altruistic), and (2) they tend to maximize their unlawful appropriations and to indulge in major usurpations of national patrimony (Pareto 1968: 59). Elite becomes decadent when its own material and short-term interests begin to outweigh the ideal and long-term interests of the community and the nation (Pareto 1966: 257–8). Even if Pareto placed more emphasis on emotional motives in elite behavior, we cannot help the impression that he implicitly admitted some kind of collective strategic intelligence that helps the ruling elite maintain a high level of circulation between superior and inferior elements and prevent its own fall. While Pareto, as mentioned above, found the fall of old ruling elites inevitable, how they lose their power is fully in their hands. Only their own wisdom or idiocy determines if this will happen in a violent way (through bloodshed and suffering) or through gradual evolutionary revitalization, as enabled by the circulation between superior and inferior elements. Pareto himself clearly preferred the latter option, referring to the ruling elites' wise ability to identify how to adopt in its own ranks all those of popular descent that are ready to form the new elite in a timely manner (Pareto 1968: 39). Elites without such a strategic intelligence are bound to fall soon. Pareto criticized the bourgeois elite for ruining themselves ignorantly by investing into the growth of the proletariat and its elites

---

35 Pareto maintains that only an open ruling elite can guarantee smooth circulation of "superior and inferior elements" between elites and masses. This circulation helps revitalize the ruling elite by offering membership to the most talented plebeian individuals, and by expulsing its least talented (inferior) members. This prevents elite "degeneration" and, at the same time, deprives masses of their (superior) individuals who might potentially lead them into fight against the ruling elite and its privileges (Pareto 1966: 131–137).

(ibid: 93). Pareto found that elites normally commit suicide (Pareto 1966: 157) by failing to identify and vigorously defend their own long-term interests. He carefully described cases of elites who lacked sufficient collective willpower and intelligence, behaved like a crowd without a leader, and watched in fascination as emerging elites gradually took their privileges.

Other elite theory classics found the elite tendency to isolate themselves from the masses a matter of course as well but associated it with completely different consequences for elite sustainability. While Pareto saw it as the beginning of the end for elites, Mosca and Michels found it to be an element of stability for the ruling (leadership) elite. Mosca sought the stability of ruling elites not only in their ability to generate a suitable ideology (formula) to legitimize their power, but also in their tendency to preserve the hereditary character of their elite positions, even under democratic circumstances. In other words, he found nepotism and clientelism very beneficial for the sustenance of democratic elites. Michels found open elite-mass relations a threat to elite leading positions as well. He found their indispensability and independence from the masses to be the principal conditions of leadership elite sustainability. As part of his skeptical view of democracy, Michels maintained that democratically elected elites can only stay in power by becoming oligarchic. The sustainability of such a democratically arisen oligarchy is threatened by "two enemy powers: the democratic resistance of the masses and... transformation into monarchy. Thus, danger from below and from its own center. Rebels on one side and usurpers on the other." (Michels 1931: 170) He found usurpers to be the greater threat. Similarly to Pareto, Michels found the sources of stability of elite-mass relations in elite intelligence: based on their great (intellectual and professional) distance from the masses, elites can always control the masses and only "overstep the mark" if something suddenly obscures their sight (Michels 1931: 150). Michels maintained that in order to most effectively defend against new aspirers for elite positions in party hierarchy, old leaders must create isolated leadership cartels (Michels 1931: 151), allowing only those who are favored by the old leaders to enter their ranks. This, however, was seen as an end to intra-party democracy by Michels. It basically left democratic elites with two choices: either stay elites at the cost of betraying democracy, or stay true to democracy and lose their elite positions. Therefore, the sustainability of democratic elites is a *contradictio in adiecto* or, more specifically, a short-term phenomenon.

Elite cohesion and independence

Post-classic elite theory scholars have tried to make elite theory compatible with democracy. Peter Bachrach (1969) called the broad stream of conceptions reconciling democracy with the existence of elites "democratic elitism". This stream was primarily represented by Joseph A. Schumpeter, Karl Mannheim, Harold D. Lasswell, Ortega y Gasset, Raymond Aron, William Kornhauser, and Suzanne Keller. All those authors as well as numerous followers realized the precarious nature of the position democratic elites permanently find themselves in. This was most clearly expressed in two frequently quoted sentences by Raymond Aron: "A unified elite means the end of freedom. But when the groups of the elite are not only distinct but become a disunity, it means the end of the State." (Aron 1950: 143) The key concepts democratic elitists used to describe a balanced elite configuration were, on one hand "moral unity", "collective identity", "compromise", "cohesion", and "solidarity", and on the other hand "differences", "differentiation", "non-violent competition", "mutual checks and balances", and "autonomy". In short, stable democracy requires that elites are cohesive, but not too much so, as well as autonomous, but only in relative terms. Again, the motive of finding the desired equilibrium between two dangerous extremes comes up. Democratic elites can only stay democratic if they maintain this equilibrium. Democratic elitists are united in their view that democratic elite sustainability is possible, yet only at the expense of somewhat reducing democracy and restricting elite openness vis-à-vis the masses. Democratic elites must preserve a high level of independence or autonomy from the popular masses in order to ensure the better functioning of democracy.

However, identifying and maintaining the right level of independence and autonomy, and of unity and differentiation, is a very difficult task. Only a sufficiently intelligent democratic elite that is aware of its long-term interests is capable of maintaining the desired state of being "united in diversity" and successfully avoiding its own gradual transformation into a rigid power pyramid or an exceedingly horizontal and impotent structure. This view basically distanced democratic elitists from Pareto's assumed elite predestination to commit suicide unknowingly. By introducing the meritocratic principle into decision making procedures, democratic elitists also distanced themselves from Mosca's nepotism and clientelism which, in their view, undermined mutual checks and balances and free competition between elites, preventing intelligent governance. According to democratic elitists, it is the intelligent use of power and the elite's awareness of their collective identity and moral duties towards the rest of society that comprise the fundamental conditions of stable democracy. Intelligent elites know this and act accordingly. Dennis Pirages, one among the U.S. post-war elitologists who inclined to democratic elitism, was convinced that elites must lack intelligence to undermine their own cohesion, which makes their authority problematic and leads to the loss of regime legitimacy (Pirages 1976). He adopted Aron's thesis that the fall of old feudal oligarchies was the result of moral decay and intra-elite quarrels, rather than progressing industrialization or an inherent inadequacy of the oligarchy in the industrial society (Aron 1968). Aron also assumed that elites must know and cooperate with each other, knowing how to combine autonomy with cooperation (Aron 1968). Similarly, Suzanne Keller thought that elite ability "to act independently and yet strive to present a united moral front" (Keller 1963: 127) is an essential condition of democratic stability. Unfortunately, neither she nor other democratic elitism scholars answered the question of how the desired unity in diversity can be attained. They did not offer any explanation of how democratic elites should intelligently balance between the dual poles of their perpetual dilemma.

Democratic elitists find competition and mutual checks and balances between elites to be the basic principles of sustaining real democracy. These can, however, only be applied in practice if elites are autonomous (Keller 1963: 273–4). Only autonomous or mutually independent elites are able to retain their democratic character so that there is meaningful competition and mutual checks and balances amongst them. The issue of elite autonomy was elaborated in most detail by Eva Etzioni-Halevy (1993: 97–9). She named her specific contribution to elite theory "demo-elitism".[36] She defined relative elite autonomy as ability of elites and sub-elites[37] to control the resources their power is based on. She is convinced that elites and sub-elites are autonomous if (a) they are not threatened of any physical coercion, (b) they are independent of other actors' material resources, (c) they are not controlled by other actors' administrative-organizational resources, and (d) their symbolic activities are independent from any outsider resources. Etzioni-Halevy views intra-elite conflicts and weak elite-public relations as specific indications of relative elite autonomy. Strong intra-elite ties facilitate backstage collusions, clientelism, and

---

36 Demo-elitism, as an independent stream of democratic elitism.
37 Medium-level, small-scale elites which include lower-level elites at the national level, such as medium-level officials in the national government administration, as well as policy makers at the regional or local levels (Etzioni-Halevy 1993: 4).

a corrupt elite symbiosis — phenomena that do not only undermine elite autonomy but also devalue the principles of representation, openness, competition, and elite mutual checks and balances that are essential for the functioning of democracy. On the other hand, strong elite-mass relations cause inadequate dependence of elites on masses and increase the risk of a populist (plebiscitary) leader arising within the elites and using the masses to change democracy into autocracy.

Democratic elitists are mostly criticized for the facts that, in their theory, elites appear too independent from masses (Ruostetsaari 2006). Their formula for a stable democracy seems to be too often reduced to the slogan: "Competing elites and passive masses." This is primarily criticized by proponents of deliberative/participative democracy (see Nekola's chapter in this book). No matter how good the democracy offered by this formula is, we cannot ignore that it is too general and too voluntarist. It gives us very little information on the contents of elite cohesion and the desired intensity thereof. We can only hypothesize that intra-elite relations must be strong enough to resist the temptations of the less intelligent elite segments to abuse power. Ultimately, all depends on elite ability and goodwill to act intelligently, i.e. to maintain internal dialogue and mutual respect. Structural factors and the masses play very little roles in this. We also do not know to what extent the required elite cohesion is compatible with the vitality of basic democratic mechanisms such as elite competition and mutual checks and balances. How can elites compete and, at the same time, be united? Democratic elitists might argue that intra-elite relations should not be as strong as to become clientelist ties. However, this is pretty much all they can argue. They have not yet studied in more detail the concept of intelligent elite capable of continuously solving the perpetual democratic elite dilemma. So far, democratic elitists have been unable to clearly delineate the golden third way which will keep elites within the bounds of desirable autonomy, on one hand, and healthy dependency, on the other hand. They cannot identify when exactly dependency becomes unhealthy or autonomy grows into an undesirable separation of elites from the public.

Elite cohesion and structural integration

C. Wright Mills saw the level of elite integration in the United States of his time as a great threat to democracy because too cohesive elites, in his view, tended to manipulate citizens and erode "the genuine public" into a mass that was unable to control elites and correct their behavior. Mills understood elite power structure as a set of hierarchically ordered circles in different parts of society that are dominated by the so-called higher circles of the power elite. Members of the higher circles in each part of society have the same origin, share the same opinions, and maintain close personal and social contacts (Mills 1966: 349). Discipline and common interest overcome their differences and tie them together even across the borders of countries at war (ibid: 336). They are characterized by psychological and social affinity, shared values, and strong class consciousness (ibid: 339). Finally, Mills explicitly mentioned the clientelist character of the power elite by stating that a person pursuing career in elite circles must be first admitted by one of the cliques inside elites, no matter what his abilities are (ibid: 408).

Thus, Mills was one of the first scholars to explicitly formulate the key role of informal networks for elite cohesion and emphasize the importance of a structured network of informal interactions in the sociological study of elite integration. Other sociologists (e.g. Domhoff 1967, Giddens 1975, Moore 1979, Useem 1984) built their conceptions of elite integration upon Mills's approach. The idea of integration circles in democratic elites—as a specific aspect of elite cohesion and integration—was taken up systematically by members of probably the most influential stream in elite theory, the "new elitism". Led by John Higley, new elitist scholars assumed that a specific configuration of democratic elites might guarantee their sustainability. Based on analyzing the history of democratic regimes, a specific elite configuration[38] might be inferred that was essential for stable democracy. New elitists tried to reformulate the perpetual dilemma of democratic elites. In their theory, the dilemma was not one between a rigid power pyramid and an amorphous horizontal structure. Instead, they analyzed elite relations in interactionist terms such as "consensus", "negotiation", "opinion distance", "ideological conflict", "integration", and "fragmentation". They tried to uncover and elaborate the different parameters of elite configuration and investigate the relationship between those parameters and democratic regime stability, for which both excessive integration and excessive fragmentation were detrimental. Fundamental was their emphasis on the differential integration and disintegration (fragmentation) of elites. Stable democracy did not require elites to be

---

38 New elitists understood the term "configuration" similarly as astronomy understood the mutual positions of planetary systems. Elite configuration was defined as "the relative position and size of elite circles (political, bureaucratic, capitalist, managerial, cultural, religious, military, etc.) in the constellation of power" (Dogan 2003: 1).

integrated in all parameters. A stable democratic elite configuration was represented by a network of interactions that were integrated in some parameters and disintegrated in other parameters. Thus, the integration/ fragmentation equilibrium was to be sought in those parameters.

According to three principal new elitism scholars, there are two basic dimensions of national elite functioning: structural integration and value consensus. Structural integration is represented by the relative inclusiveness of formal and informal communication and influence networks between persons, groups, and fractions of the national elite. Value consensus means relative agreement between those persons, groups, and fractions about formal and informal rules and codes of political conduct and about the usefulness of political institutions (Field, Higley and Burton 1990). Only integrated elites guarantee democratic stability. A consensual configuration of democratic elites is ideal for sustainability. In this configuration, elites are both consensually united and structurally integrated. However, this is not a hierarchic integration. Consensually united elites are structurally integrated in an inclusive way that goes across individual fractions, with neither fraction dominating. Value consensus is also inclusive, with individual fractions opposing each other publicly on ideological and public policy issues.

To what extent is the above consensual elite configuration similar to Mills's united elite model? How long can elite opinion and social diversity last in an environment of strong confidence and mutual ties? New elitists provide the following answer to those questions. Democratic elites should not exist in the form of strongly interdependent elite members enclosed in a relatively small group of the powerful. Democratic elites exist as network configurations of plural elite influence circles that are formed around and across institutions and policy issues. Elite influence circles are based on repeated interactions between elite members who share similar interests and want to solve similar policy issues (Higley et al. 1991: 37). The relativization of centralized decision-making is an essential characteristic of this concept. While this model of network relations has a relatively centralized interaction structure, it lacks a permanent group of leaders. Moreover, no network member knows the real boundaries and composition of these elite circles. No one knows exactly who is and who is not a member. Everyone knows only those he/she interacts with. Nevertheless, some members are more important than others because they are more closely linked to other important influence circles and other similarly important persons in the network. Those members belong to the more specialized circles and are typically active about several issues in several arenas simultaneously. They form a kind of super-network which is hierarchically above other networks because it is the most influential, but it has no center. New elitists often refer to it as "the elite central circle". It helps change and prioritize decisions and constitutes a key communication structure for negotiating exchanges, compromises, and informal understandings without which the broadly diversified national elite would soon break into competing fractions (ibid: 37–8). The elite central circle ensures the sharing of power by different elite segments. It is predominantly based on informal integration which ensures that interests of all elite fractions are realized. By allowing members of one elite segment to access members of other segments in a relatively easy and informal way, it facilitates the stability of democracy (ibid: 50).

The structural integration of the Czech elites

Ever since the 1950s, grave controversies have existed over the nature of the power elites have in modern society. The questions have been: Does the democratic elitism model work in the practice of Western societies? Is there a real competition for political leadership in which elites apply checks and balances to each other? Are elites in the process of power concentration, or rather power fragmentation? Do elites comprise a relatively coherent power group (Mills 1966) or rather a plurality of different veto groups with competing power interests (Riesman 1961, Dahl 1961)? Are ruling democratic elites enjoying a great deal of autonomy (capable of doing what they want), or are they rather fatally dependent on the opinions and wishes of other elites or the general public? In this respect, what is the situation in Czech society? How successful has Czech society been in its maneuvering between the dual extremes of omnipotent/powerless elites, i.e. between the Scylla of cohesive elites with the resulting oligarchy, and the Charybdis of intra-elite relations breakdown with the resulting risk of demagogic leader autocracy? As we suggested above, the identification and maintenance of equilibrium between the two extremes requires that we know the levels of elite social cohesion, openness, independence, and integration.

In the light of the new elitist typology of elites, the Czech elites are considered consensual (Higley and Lengyel 2000: 15). This assessment is based on a few simple facts: ever since the fall of communism, the Czech elites have been able to agree on the democratic rules of political practice, have respected those rules, and have avoided any serious excesses of right-wing or left-wing political extremism. All this has coincided with clearly identifiable democratic stability in the Czech Republic over the past twenty years. However, these simple facts pertain to political elites, rather than relations between the individual elite segments, and therefore, indicate value consensus rather than elite structural integration. They do not indicate whether the Czech elites have a tendency to increase cohesion or whether their level of structural integration is critically high, thus jeopardizing their sustainability as democratic elites. These facts also do not provide answers for the questions whether the Czech elite central circle is broad and inclusive enough, whether or not it has a center, and to what extent it is or is not dominated by one of the elite fractions or segments. The assessment of the Czech elites as consensually united based on the above facts is practically an ex-post assessment. However, if elite theory wants to play a more important role in explaining social events, its arguments should rest on indicators with predictive power.

Mutual trust and contacts

Since the issue of value/opinion consensus is addressed by the Prudký and Tuček chapters within this book, we will focus on analyzing the structural integration of the Czech elites, based on the concept of elite influence circles. In our 2007 quantitative survey of the Czech elites,[39] we focused on three variables describing democratic elite structural integration that, in our opinion, comprise the essential circumstances for their sustainability. Those variables included: density of mutual contacts between the different elite segments; mutual trust and influence within elites; and dependence of the different elite segments on other segments. Data analysis will enable us to identify the size of the elite central circle in the Czech Republic and its composition from different elite segments. We assume that each elite segment creates an interconnected network with three basic integration levels or circles:

---

39 The survey was conducted by the Center for Social and Economic Strategies, Faculty of Social Sciences, Charles University in Prague (CESES), under the title "The Elite-Public Relations", within the framework of the Faculty of Social Sciences Research Objective. Field data collection took place in autumn 2007 on a sample of 1035 respondents in high formal positions within political (111 respondents), public administration (138 respondents), security (77 respondents), economic (260 respondents), media (97 respondents), cultural (arts, education and research, churches, 158 respondents), and civic sector (204 respondents) institutions. The following chapter by Milan Tuček includes more details on the survey.

(1) the network core, i.e. the central circle,
(2) the semi-periphery, whose members partially belong to both the central circle and the periphery, and
(3) the periphery, whose members clearly do not belong to the central circle.

Members of each elite network may at a given time find themselves in one of the following three positions: (1) insiders (members of the central circle), (2) members of the semi-periphery, or (3) outsiders (periphery members). We believe that the integration structure of positions within the elite network as a whole can be described in similar terms. The relative membership size between the different integration circles will be used to characterize the specific structural integration of both the individual elite segments and the elite as a whole.

Since elite networks are characterized by trust (they should be more than just complicity networks relying mostly on fear), individual members' central or peripheral positions will depend not only on the density (frequency) of their contacts with other network members, but also the trust they hold for other network holders. Trust and contact frequency between members describe the level and quality of a network's structural integration. The more trust and contacts the given elite network has, the higher its level of structural integration. Therefore, those elite members with dense contacts[40] and high levels of trust for other elite members comprise the elite core and are defined as **insiders** — members of the given elite network's central circle. In contrast, **outsiders** with rare contacts and low trust are located in the elite network's periphery. Two types of members comprise the semi-periphery:

(a) **conspirers:** their contact density would qualify them for central circle membership but they do not hold trust for members of the central circle, and therefore, they rather form a foreign element and their persuasion pulls them out to the network's periphery, and
(b) **aspirers:** they are attracted by the network core's gravity, hold high levels of trust for its members, but their rare contacts with those members do not allow them to become full members of the network core.

As suggested above, in order to interpret the character of any given network's structural integration, we must identify the size of each integration circle, i.e. the relative proportions of insiders, conspirers, aspirers, and outsiders in total membership. We may reasonably

---

40 We define dense contacts as those activated at least once monthly.

assume that a broader central circle tends to facilitate communication, negotiation, and reciprocity between the different elite segments, and thus enhances structural integration. In contrast, relatively higher numbers of periphery members (outsiders) will result in lower levels of network integration. In general, the narrower the central insider circle and the broader the outsider circle, the more oligarchic a network. Networks with more outsiders than insiders reflect the oligarchic type of elite structural integration and, in contrast, networks with more insiders than outsiders reflect the democratic integration type.

Table 2.1: Distribution of network positions within elite segments

Elite segment	Proportion of elite positions (per cent)				Total	In/Out ratio	Respon-dents
	Insider	Conspirer	Aspirer	Outsider			
Politics	15	18	20	48	100	0.3	111
Economics	31	13	28	29	100	1.1	260
Public administration	31	21	22	27	100	1.1	128
Media	13	20	23	44	100	0.3	97
Culture	23	1	70	6	100	3.7	158
Security	13	6	38	44	100	0.3	77
Civic sector	31	5	48	16	100	2.0	204

Source: CESES 2007.

Note: Elite positions were identified as a combination of two variables: frequency of contacts with members of the given elite segment and level of trust between them. Respondents were divided into two groups according to contact frequency: those with occasional or no contacts (K1) and those with at least one contact monthly (K2). Similarly, two trust groups were created based on Question 48: one group comprised of those who strongly distrust or rather distrust (D1) and the other of those who strongly trust or rather trust (D2). Missing answers and don't knows were assigned to the first groups, i.e. those with little contact frequency and little trust, respectively. Subsequently, an aggregate variable describing network position was created, distinguishing between insiders (K2 and D2), conspirers (K2 and D1), aspirers (K1 and D2) and outsiders (K1 and D1). This procedure was performed based on available data on mutual relations between elites and does not provide an insight as detailed as traditional network analysis. On the other hand, we consider it fruitful and justified for our purposes (see above). Full question wordings: Question 42, "I am going to read out several elite groups. Could you please tell me how often you are in contact with their members, no matter if it is a personal, telephonic, or written contact", and Question 48, "Do you have trust for the following groups of people?", with the following answer options for both questions: "(a) high ranking politicians, (b) managers in large corporations, (c) high ranking public administration officials, (d) high ranking media workers (TV, radio, newspapers, and advertising), (e) high ranking science workers, (f) high ranking police officials, (g) top members of important voluntary and non-profit organizations.

The following Table describes the character of structural integration within the different Czech elite segments by looking at the relative sizes of their network central circles, semi-peripheries, and peripheries. Each element of this structure is represented by a given number of members sharing a specific position within their "home" network.

Elites in the areas of security, media, and politics have the lowest proportions of insiders, and thus, represent the least open, most oligarchic type of structural integration. The structure of these elite segments resembles a pyramid with a broad foundation of peripheral and semi-peripheral members below and a narrow tip of central circle members above them. Most members have rare contacts with or do not trust the insiders (except for the security elites with "only" half of their members not trusting their colleagues). At the opposite extreme, the civic, economic, and administrative elites represent the wide open, democratic type of structural integration. They have the broadest central circles of all elite segments, including about 30% of their respective membership; broad semi-peripheries; and relatively narrow groups of outsiders. The cultural (education, science, arts, etc.) elites are specific for their rather democratic type of structural integration with very narrow outsider groups, very broad semi-peripheries (almost 100% of which are aspirers) and relatively large groups of insiders. This specific structure is probably related to the network's heterogeneous composition, with three different areas whose representatives trust each other but do not maintain close contacts.

The asymmetric composition of the semi-periphery in favor of the trusting aspirers is not only typical for the cultural elites, but also for the civic, security, and economic elites. The total advantage of aspirers over conspirers suggests that members of the different networks tend to trust each other more often than they get in contact with each other. However, trust is very important for establishing contacts as well. Members of the civic elite trust each other the most frequently (80%). More trust than distrust is also typical for the economic (59%), administrative (53%) and security elites (51%). Members of the political (36%) and media (35%) elites trust each other the least. Dense contacts are only characteristic for the administrative elite and, to some extent, the economic elite. About one-third of the political, media, and civic elites declare dense contacts. The security and, rather surprisingly, the cultural elites declare the lowest contact density.

Typically, elites with the oligarchic type of structural integrations (the media and the political elites) have relatively high proportions of conspirers, i.e. supporters of a kind of "internal opposition" to the loyal central circle

Table 2.2: Positions within the networks of individual elite segments by elite segment membership

Elite segment	Network position	Elite segment (column percentages)							Total
		POL	PA	SEC	ECO	MED	CUL	CIV	
Politics (POL)	Insider	56	23	26	3	7	9	7	15
	Conspirer	29	22	16	9	25	17	15	18
	Aspirer	9	21	22	34	13	15	15	20
	Outsider	6	34	37	54	55	58	64	47
	Total	100	100	100	100	100	100	100	100
Public administration (PA)	Insider	51	53	62	17	18	25	20	31
	Conspirer	29	20	8	17	23	28	21	21
	Aspirer	10	19	20	37	14	23	18	22
	Outsider	11	9	10	30	45	24	41	27
	Total	100	100	100	100	100	100	100	100
Security (SEC)	Insider	16	17	55	5	15	7	5	13
	Conspirer	7	9	3	5	7	3	6	6
	Aspirer	42	43	33	41	26	42	33	38
	Outsider	35	31	9	49	53	49	57	44
	Total	100	100	100	100	100	100	100	100
Economics (ECO)	Insider	39	15	25	54	34	23	13	31
	Conspirer	14	22	9	9	15	12	13	13
	Aspirer	24	30	32	24	27	31	30	28
	Outsider	23	33	33	13	24	34	44	29
	Total	100	100	100	100	100	100	100	100
Media (MED)	Insider	10	8	12	7	56	7	10	13
	Conspirer	38	17	20	1	26	25	12	20
	Aspirer	8	15	17	35	12	22	28	23
	Outsider	44	60	51	44	6	4	50	45
	Total	100	100	100	100	100	100	100	100
Culture (CUL)	Insider	28	23	22	16	25	48	9	23
	Conspirer	1	1	0	2	0	1	1	1
	Aspirer	69	73	75	72	74	43	82	70
	Outsider	3	3	3	11	1	8	8	6
	Total	100	100	100	100	100	100	100	100
Civic sector (CIV)	Insider	37	26	32	12	40	28	50	31
	Conspirer	7	5	6	5	4	5	5	5
	Aspirer	44	47	43	61	43	51	38	48
	Outsider	11	22	19	23	12	16	7	16
	Total	100	100	100	100	100	100	100	100

Source: CESES 2007

members. The security elites form an exception that can only be explained by the hierarchical, i.e. undemocratic structure of the security institutions, which must be found natural by their top management members. Higher proportions of "internal opposition" in the media and political networks are probably related to the fact that their members are more often engaged in opposing political fractions. The relatively high proportion (21%) of mistrustful conspirers, indicating a tendency of narrowing central circle, is also typical for the democratically integrated administrative elites, suggesting this type of integration is rater fragile. In crisis or if members of the central circle lose confidence, conspirers may easily become outsiders, and as a result, the integration character of the bureaucratic elites may become predominantly oligarchic. This distinguishes the administrative elites from other democratically integrated elites, in which we have observed a high stability of the democratic integration type and a clear tendency to expand the central circle.

Now we will address the question to what extent the Czech elites are integrated as a whole. First we will take a look at the overlap (in terms of contacts and trust) between the individual elite segments and other segments' central circles or semi-peripheries. The following Table confirms the expectation that elites are most strongly integrated within the individual segments, i.e. in their "homes". The level of structural integration between elite segments is differentiated. In one part, elite networks are highly integrated, and in the rest, they are rather fragmented.

The political, administrative, and security elites appear to be the most narrowly interconnected. Their central circles have the largest overlaps. The so-called power elites (the political, administrative, security, and economic segments) in the Czech Republic do not form one integrated bloc. This is because the economic elites are not part of such a bloc. The power of money they represent is thus largely separated from government power, as represented by officials and politicians. The central circle of the economic segment is relatively isolated. Membership in this circle is strongly reserved to members of the economic and, partially, the political elites. The economic elites maintain much less contacts with politics and the public administration but aspire to membership in their central circles. This means that the economic elites are being isolated by the government elites, rather than isolating themselves from them. In short, politicians and officials do not allow businesspeople and managers to access their networks' central circles as often as the latter might want. The fact that government power strives to protect itself from the power of money is likeable but, on the other hand, we know that this protection is likely to be selective. Government networks open up to those businesspeople who offer the most or can be blackmailed. Therefore, it is not easy to tell whether the power of money is controlled by state power or vice versa. However, the Czech general public clearly believes that this affair is mutual, representing a corrupt symbiosis between members of the power elite, i.e. officials, politicians, and businesspeople alike.[41]

The civic sector elites are largely isolated from the power elite network, suggesting they act as society's counter-elite. On the other hand, they clearly tend to integrate more frequently with members of the public administration and politicians, relative to members of the economic elite. This means that the civic elites are integrated into the power networks through grants and public procurement, rather than philanthropy and sponsorship. The media and the cultural elites find themselves in the periphery of the other networks, and show no strong aspirations to become insiders in the power networks. Overall, the so-called influence elites (the media, cultural, and civic segments) are relatively weakly connected to each other, remain fragmented, and do not seem to form any focused oppositional bloc vis-à-vis the power elites. On the other hand, they are clearly strongly isolated from the political, administrative, and security elites' power block. The overall integration of the Czech elites is thus characterized by the dominant position of the power elites around the government, on one hand, and the fragmented and inferior position of the influence elites on the other hand.

What is the size of the core transelite network, which connects the different elite segment networks and guarantees the functioning of the entire society? Is there one? And if so, what is it composed of? In trying to answer these questions, we will depart from the well-known idea of Michael Useem, who made an "inner circle" position within the corporate elite contingent upon multiple memberships in the management boards of different corporations. In short, members of the inner circle have good contacts and enjoy trust from other corporations than their own, which translates into their management board functions. Analogously, we may define central circle members as those respondents who maintain close contacts with other networks and, at the same time, trust them, i.e. they are insiders within those networks. If core transelite network membership is defined as insider status in most, i.e. at least four elite networks out of seven, the central circle comprises of 17% of the total elite network members. It is surrounded by a broad semi-periphery

---

41   See Milan Tuček's chapter below.

Table 2.3: Overlaps between insiders of the different networks

Elite segment	Elite segment (column percentages)						Civic sector
	Politics	Public administration	Security	Economics	Media	Culture	
Politics	**56**	23	26	3	7	9	*7*
Public administration	**51**	**53**	**62**	17	18	25	20
Security	16	17	**55**	5	15	7	5
Economics	**39**	15	25	**54**	**34**	23	13
Media	10	8	12	7	**56**	7	10
Culture	28	23	22	16	25	**48**	9
Civic sector	**37**	26	**32**	12	**40**	28	**50**

Source: CESES 2007.

Note: Overlaps with more than 30% of insiders are in bold, overlaps with 10% or less are in italics. The authors have defined those margins for better orientation within the table.

with half of the total membership and a strong advantage of aspirers over conspirers.[42] The periphery is comprised of about one-third of membership, i.e. almost 50% more people than the central circle. This means that the structural integration of the Czech elites as a whole is oligarchic, rather than democratic. The total structural integration tends to follow the oligarchic model even if conspirers are added to the insiders they maintain dense contacts with.

Table 2.4: Transelite network integration circles

Network position	Per cent
Insider	17
Conspirer	11
Aspirer	39
Outsider	33
Total	100

Source: CESES 2007.

---

42 Conspirers are defined here as those elite network members who are insiders in most elite segments but have only little trust for most of them. In contrast, aspirers are not insiders in most elite segments but trust most of them. Transelite network outsiders are defined as members who are not insiders in most networks and do not trust most of them.

The different elite segments have different representations in the central circle, with the political elites clearly dominating and the civic elites being the least represented.

Table 2.5: Composition of the transelite network central circle

Elite segment	Per cent
Politics	20
Public administration	14
Security	13
Economics	14
Media	15
Culture	14
Civic sector	9
Total	100

Source: CESES 2007.

In this respect, we must point out two important facts. The relatively little — less than expected — representation of the administrative elites within the central circle is to some extent caused by the facts that they include not only high ranking public administration officials but also judges, public prosecutors, and representatives of supervisory bodies (Supreme Audit Office, Office for the Protection of Competition), who either consider relations with politics and other elites a threat to their own independence and try to minimize them, or at least do not mention such relations in surveys like ours.[43] In contrast, the relatively and absolutely high representation of security elites is to some extent determined by the fact that network membership has been constructed as frequency of contacts between one elite segment and the other elites, as relayed by members of that segment. Clearly, the frequency of contacts segment A claims to maintain with segment B should be approximately equal to the frequency segment B states for segment A. This, however, is not true for the security elites. While the security elites state very frequent contacts with the other elites, the other elites describe their contacts with them as the least frequent. This may mean that members of the security elite have nominated themselves into the central network, and this fact has to be borne in mind in interpreting the results.

---

43   See e.g. Frič 2007.

The nature and strength of informal ties

According to new elitists, elite structural integration is primarily based on informal ties connecting elite members in terms of trust and reciprocity. However, not all elite members are connected to others through equally strong ties and not all of them are equally capable of creating, maintaining, or enhancing those ties. We assume that members of the central circle (insiders) have achieved their superior network position through skills as well as social capital, including networking and brokering. Networking is defined as building or developing interpersonal contacts with people who are willing to help if necessary and expect the same in return. Brokering is a special form of networking in that help in solving a specific problem is ensured by mediating contacts to other network members, rather than provided directly. Acquaintances are contacted on behalf of other acquaintances who need help. Brokering as an indirect aid technique is an integral part of the role of central elite network members. A substantially higher level of brokering activities may indicate that an insider really is an important elite network member. Members of the elite central network thus should be networking champions. They should display high levels of brokering because they are pushed by members of the semi-periphery and periphery to help them and their acquaintances. We may assume that the more central network position a member takes, the more frequently he is confronted with requests for help by other network members and the more frequently he has to prove his position justified by acting as a "useful acquaintance". In turn, members of the network periphery may be expected to display the lowest levels of brokering.

We operationalize brokers as those elite network members who at least once a month help their acquaintances solve their (personal or professional) problems.[44] Our analysis confirms that members of the central network indeed broker much more frequently than elite network periphery members. Typically, this is related to contact frequency, rather than trust in the different elite segments. Aspirers tend to broker

---

44 The variable was constructed as a combination of both items in Question 41, i.e. help with professional as well as personal problems. A broker is defined as someone who helps with one or the other type of problem at least once a month. Full wording of Question 41: "People may also solve their problems informally, i.e. through family, friends, and acquaintances working in public offices or other institutions. How often do you (a) help another person solve work-related issues by acting as their acquaintance? (b) help another person solve personal issues by acting as their acquaintance?"

much less than conspirers, who display even higher levels of brokering than insiders. In principle, the important positions of central network members come along with their brokering activities. Another important finding is that brokering strongly facilitates the positions of conspirers within the semi-periphery, thus making the semi-periphery hierarchic. Conspirers appear more important than aspirers in terms of elite structural integration.

The question remains of to what extent brokering indicates levels of isolation or autonomy in the different elite networks. Very open networks do not need brokers because almost everyone has contact with everyone else and is able to ask for help directly. Therefore, higher levels of brokering suggest isolated networks and the necessity for brokers to facilitate contacts between them. On the other hand, very open networks would simultaneously be too dependent of each other and a low level of brokering may suggest low elite autonomy. The total proportion of brokers among the Czech elites is approximately one-third (31%). This, however, can hardly be interpreted as indicating that the different elites are rather open and dependent on each other. Indeed, we do not know the specific relationship between brokering level and the desirable level of elite network autonomy.

Table 2.6: Relationship between network position and brokering

N = 983, percentages	Insider	Conspirer	Aspirer	Outsider	Total
Brokers	46	49	26	22	31
Non-Brokers	54	51	74	78	69
Total	100	100	100	100	100

Source: CESES 2007.

Networking literature (e.g. Baker 1994, Stanley 1993) advises everyone seeking success in any field to invest time and energy into networking. Those aspiring to success in business, academia, NGOs, or public administration should actively build their personal networks, rather than remain the passive objects of other people's networking. Networking has become normal part of business management and, more generally, capitalist competition. Networking capabilities have become standard parts of both individual and collective social capital. In spite of the fact that social capital scholars have paid little attention to networking, it is clear that people in Western countries generally accept it as a positive facilitator of collaboration and market economy. Networking is used openly and on a mass scale in those countries.

The networking situation is quite different in transforming post-communist countries. The transformation from socialism to capitalism generated a great deal of social disorganization, along with high insecurity, and elites in those countries tried to overcome that through enhanced networking. Naturally, the former communist nomenclature elites had the greatest chances in this effort. They had the most advanced personal networks in place and, moreover, were best trained in networking at this level. Under the communist regime, the leading cadres had to pay little attention to the substance of what they led, as the ability to know "the right people above" and use them to one's benefit was more important. When the communist party was toppled, those people's networks persevered in the disorganized public administration institutions as well as government run/sponsored businesses, often dominating them as the only well-functioning forms of coordination. However, the old elites never envisaged ending the disorganization of formal institutions, and instead, sought to use it for rent-seeking and ensuring their own subsistence. There is no doubt that it was precisely the nomenclature cadre networks who, at least for some time, became the winners of social transformation. More problematically, they left behind large numbers of people hurt by their networking activities, i.e. transformation losers. This was the source of the negative connotations networking received in post-communist countries and the ensuing popular syndrome of network/networking demonization. Another source was the fact that networking activities were often equalled to clientelism or the predatory networks of the communist regime. The unpopular character of networking as a wrongful activity in the Czech Republic is further illustrated by the fact that the term "lobbying" has predominantly negative connotations in the eyes of the general public. Networking is little popular and receives little open support from the Czech general public. The general belief is that informal relations between elite members are too strong and harmful for both democracy and the economy.[45]

What is the nature and strength of the influence of informal relations within the different elite networks? We assume a direct relationship between the strength of intra-network informal relations and the level of network isolation. The stronger are the informal relations within a given network, the higher is its isolation from potential new members trying to

---

penetrate its structure. Data analysis in Table 2.8 below reveals that the political elites perceive the highest pressure of informal relations within their own elite segment. On average, they rate the influence of their own informal networks between "very strong" and "quite strong". Also the media elites perceive "quite strong" influence of internal informal relations on their elite segment. Other elite segments rate the influence of internal informal networks as "rather strong", on average. This finding suggests that the different elite segment networks are rather isolated, with the political elite and, to some extent, the media elite feeling the most isolated.

Despite the general tendency to demonize informal networks and recognition of the strength of informal relations within the different elite segment networks, most elite respondents do not rate the orientation of informal networks as entirely contrary to the public interest. Two-fifths of respondents find informal networks within their own segments beneficial to the public, and less than one-fifth (18%) consider their orientation egoistic. The Czech elites admit the existence of "predatory elite" networks within their ranks but clearly do not demonize informal networks and their influence on society. Most of them do not believe in the popular conspiracy scenario that informal networks forge backstage deals, casting doubt upon formal procedures within the institutions those elite members run. They interpret informal elite contacts as useful networking, rather than dangerous clientelism.

Table 2.7: Perceived orientations of informal networks within own elite segment

N = 947, percentages	Own interest	Half-and-half	General interest
Security	7	46	47
Civic sector	12	30	58
Politics	16	41	43
Public administration	18	44	38
Culture	18	40	42
Media	21	46	33
Economics	24	52	24
Total	18	42	40

Note: Only respondents stating that informal networks exist within their segment are included.

Source: CESES 2007.

Table 2.8: Perceived strength of informal influence and dependence between elite segments

Elite segment	POL	PA	SEC	ECO	MED	CUL	CIV
Politics	2.05	3.35	4.27	3.62	3.53	3.99	3.89
Public administration	3.38	3.53	4.81	4.37	4.21	4.47	4.44
Security	2.69	3.11	3.37	4.23	4.16	4.29	4.60
Economics	4.16	4.05	5.08	3.15	4.24	4.56	4.92
Media	4.04	4.46	5.01	4.13	2.90	4.79	4.63
Culture, science	3.76	3.31	5.04	4.17	3.95	3.38	4.24
Civic sector	3.48	3.28	4.68	3.94	3.66	4.49	3.20

Note: Values represent arithmetic means of answers to the question, "How strong is the informal influence on the orientation of the domain you belong to, of the following", followed by a list of elite segments. Answer scale: 1 = very strong, 2 = quite strong, 3 = rather strong, 4 = rather weak, 5 = minimum, 6 = none.

Source: CESES 2007.

To what extent are the different elite segments dependent upon other segment networks? How do the different elite segments rate the strength of external informal relations and how is the strength of their own influence rated by other elite segments? Has the informal pressure from outside grown into an unhealthy dependence of one elite type upon another? If we define dependence as informal external influence that is perceived within the given elite segment as "rather strong", we can say that independence between the different elite segment networks is perceived much more frequently than dependence. Informal relations between the different elite segments are mostly rather weak to minimum. Most elite segments find themselves rather independent of the other elites. All elite segments perceive the influence of their own internal informal relations, on average, as stronger than that of external informal relations. However, this perception may be reverse in individual cases. The security elites are the main exception. The strength of their relations with politics highly exceeds the strength of internal relations within their own segment. The administrative elites are similarly dependent on the political elite network, rating their external relations with politicians as stronger than their own informal networks. The third case of dependence is represented by the relations between the cultural and the administrative elites. Members of the cultural elites are slightly more likely to rate the informal influence of administrative elites as higher than that of their own networks. The political, security, and civic elites find themselves dependent rather than independent.

The political elites form the only elite segment whose influence in other segments is found rather strong, on average, and at the same time, is rather strongly dependent upon other elite segments. (Politicians are perceived by outsiders as influential and they perceive strong influence from the outside.) Politicians see their segment most affected by the power (administrative and economic) elites as well as the media elites. In turn, they exercise strong influence upon the security, civic, and cultural elites. The political elites' pattern of informal influence combined with dependence is hardly surprising. However, their highest dependence rating among all elite segments seems to contradict the fact that they are considered the most influential elites of all. Therefore, the political elites are found the most informally influential and, at the same time, consider themselves the most dependent elite segment in the Czech Republic. It is difficult to tell whether this "enslaved monster" paradox reflects the political elite's real situation or rather its self-stylization into the role of

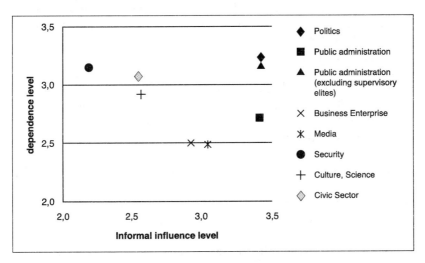

Figure 2.1: Distribution of informal influence and dependence among elites

Source: CESES 2007.

Note: Average ratings of elite informal influence, excluding intra-segment ratings (e.g. the influence of political elites upon politics is not considered). For easier interpretation, the scale has been reversed so that higher values represent higher levels of informal influence (the X axis) or dependence (the Y axis).

martyrs patiently bearing the pressure from others. At any account, we have to acknowledge the fact that politicians declare to be trapped in the demands of other elites. On the other hand, the higher level of isolation within their structural integration as a result of a relatively narrow central circle and strong intra-network relations suggest a relatively important role of stylization.

Strong influence and weak dependence represent the second pattern of informal influence/dependence. This pattern is characteristic of the administrative elites, making them the only "hegemons" of the Czech elite informal world. They are perceived by outsiders as very influential networks and perceive weak pressure from the other networks. The "rather strong" influence of the political elites, as perceived by the administrative elites, represents the only exception. This confirms the above finding that the administrative and the political elites are closely interconnected. The administrative elites and politicians form influential informal networks that strongly influence not only their own segments but also the security, the civic sector, and science and culture. The relatively weak dependence of the administrative elites seemingly contradicts their dense contacts with the political elites. As already mentioned, the administrative segment also includes the so-called supervisory elites, i.e. judges, public prosecutors, and members of central supervisory bodies who, by the definition of their offices, are motivated to claim independence. If we leave them out of the analysis, the rest of the administrative elites will lose their hegemony and fall into a similar position as the political elites, i.e. strong influence combined with strong dependence. Therefore, only the supervisory elites are the real hegemons of the Czech elite network.

Average to low influence combined with a relatively high independence of the other elites — the "freelancer pattern" — represent the third pattern of influence/dependence. It is characteristic of the economic and media elites. Even if their informal influence is mostly average, it is perceived as "rather strong" by members of the political and civic sector elites.

The last pattern of elite influence/dependence comprises of a combination of weak influence and high dependence and is typical for the security and civic elites, and to a large extent for the cultural elites. Their informal networks are at the very bottom of influence ratings and their dependence on other elite informal networks rates among the highest. From a reciprocal perspective, they are the greatest losers of the Czech elite informal networks. They find themselves at the periphery of the elite relations structure. Their situation is similar to that of the security elites who, as a result of drastic cuts in military spending, a declining weapons industry, and frequent police reforms, are totally dependent on politicians and officials. Weak influence, high dependence, generally little chances to reach consensus (Bachrach 1969: 59) and relatively low levels of contact density within the cultural elites underline the fact that "the power of diplomas" does not counterbalance the power of government elites in the Czech Republic.

Discussion

Are the levels of integration/cohesion and fragmentation balanced in the Czech elites? Do they guarantee, or rather jeopardize democracy? How does the Czech elite central circle work? Does it help change and prioritize decisions and does it constitute a key communication structure for negotiating exchange, compromise, and informal understanding in the ways new elitists would expect? Let us repeat the new elitist three basic conditions which guarantee the proper functioning of the elite central circle and prevent favorable levels of structural integration from turning into undesirable dependence or isolation. First, the central circle should be sufficiently broad and inclusive. Second, no single faction within the elite network should dominate. Third, the elite central circle should not have any clear core. The fulfillment of these three conditions comprises the new elitist instruction for democratic elites to maintain equilibrium between too high/too low structural integration/cohesion, and remain in power. Do the Czech elites follow this instruction? Do they fulfill the three conditions for a democratically functioning elite central circle? Do the above findings provide clear answers to these questions?

Let us now briefly summarize what we have found out about the Czech elites' structural integration. First, we know that the central circle of the Czech transelite network is relatively small and isolated. Contrary to the democratic ideal, an oligarchic pattern prevails in elite structural integration. This contrast may systematically distort the functioning of the central circle as the Czech democratic elite communication mechanism. Second, the transelite interaction network has a clear core, which comprises of the political and administrative elites. Those have the highest overlaps of insiders. Nevertheless, this core does not have enough gravity to receive trust from other elites (except from the economic segment). Third, the alliance of the government (political and administrative) elites appears dominant within the transelite network.

Members of the two segments display the highest density of mutual contacts, the highest interdependence, and the strongest influence on other elites. On the other hand, the different elite networks appear, on average, autonomous rather than dependent on other networks. Fourth, the government elite alliance has no competitor. The civic elites, who are expected to guard democracy, have little influence on other elites, and are more dependent, mainly on the administrative elites.[46]

The above findings are to a great extent contradictory to the democratic concept of elite structural integration.[47] A more important question is, however, whether such a pattern of elite structural integration is normal for elite cohesion in representative democracies. Would a democrat expect such a picture or would it be a bad surprise? What if it is, after all, completely natural that power elites are more influential than the cultural and civic elites? What if it is normal in a parliamentary democracy that the political and administrative elites maintain closer contacts, based on their functions, and the influence elites are separated from the power elites in order to act as a critical opposition? Clearly, not a single real democracy has so far reached the ideal elite structural integration, and reality always differs from this ideal. In our case, the reality leans towards oligarchy. It is important to know how substantial or risky such a leaning is.

If we looked at the situation through the lens of strong/weak relations that is, for example, used in the works of Etzioni-Halevy, we would have to say that the existence of strong relations between officials and politicians is no good indicator for democracy. Rather than relatively autonomous elites, we would be dealing with an undemocratic cartel. We would have to agree with the general public's conspiracy scenario that the influential elite circles control the situation from behind the scenes. Unless their interests are at stake, they let peripheral network members wage grave opinion conflicts, with spectacular media coverage underlining their ritual conflict character. Meanwhile, powerful elite members behind the scenes remain undisturbed within their cohesive complicity circles. While communist elites pretended unity and silenced their conflicts, the

---

46 This is a result of their strong dependence on grants from the government budget that are distributed by administrative officials through often barely transparent mechanisms. Civic sector dependence is further exacerbated by the fact that grants are usually appropriated for one-year periods, a fact that keeps non-profit organizations in permanent insecurity.

47 It remains a matter of debate whether this central circle really is insufficiently broad, whether correct indicators have been used to identify the network core, or whether the administrative/political elite alliance really is large enough to signify a grave conflict with the democratic pattern of structural integration.

democratic elites feign conflict and mask their cohesion. Nevertheless, we believe that our data do not justify such strong conclusions — but neither do they contradict them. Our findings mean that the Czech elites are undergoing a slow oligarchic transformation, departing from the ideal of democracy. It is, however, difficult to tell how far they have proceeded in this direction. Also unclear is whether there is a critical point in the oligarchization process beyond which elites are bound to become too dependent and isolated, departing from the democratic ideal for good.

The concept of structural integration as presented by the new elitism does not enable us to identify the exact level of threat to the position of democratic elites and democracy in the Czech Republic or predict the exact time horizon for the sustainability of contemporary elites. New elitists are little concerned with the possibility that the elite central circle would pervert into a cemented "winner takes all" coalition and quietly change democracy into oligarchy. While they realize that "elite settlements"[48] across the different elite segments help create a relatively stable elite cartel, they find this situation bound to go away without slowing the development of democracy (Burton and Higley 1998: 47–8). However, such a conclusion seems too optimistic and lacks empirical verification in the democratic practice of post-communist societies. It puts too much emphasis on elite strategic intelligence, i.e. self-restraint, an assumption criticized by as early as Pareto. Moreover, it is in conflict with the new elitist normative requirement that elite members nurture elitist values, including the duty to facilitate elite consensus and unity (Field and Higley 1980: 90–1).[49] This position draws new elitism close to democratic elitism which makes the assumption of intelligent action part of elites' very collective identity.

Above all, we would like to argue that the consensual elite and structural integration model lacks any non-elite correctives (by the masses or the general public). New elitism and democratic elitism alike do not rely on non-elite intelligence or political culture to ensure stability of the democratic regime. The cohesion and sustainability of democratic elites are their "internal affairs". For new elitists, elites should maintain closer ties with other elites rather than those parts of non-elites they represent. This is, of course, an elitist assumption, as may be expected from elite theory. However, we find it important to know—not only in today's situation of the Czech elites — to what extent the general public

---

48 Elite settlements are much more fundamental events than elite pacts.
49 This requirement was later reformulated as the imperative of "unity in diversity" (Higley and Lengyel 2000: 4–5).

can be expected to correct elite behavior. As suggested by Chapter 1, the Czech situation is dangerous precisely because the Czech general public acts in a relatively resigned way and simultaneously maintains a quasi-opposition to its elites. It neither recognizes their authority nor openly rebels against them.[50] Under these circumstances, elites have reasons to despise their citizens. This motivates unwise attitudes and makes elites balance between the extremes of excessive isolation and mutual dependence. While it is difficult to identify the relationship between the strong intra-elite relations on one hand, and clientelism and cronyism on the other, we may say that the Czech elites as democratic elites do not act wisely enough to prevent long-term conspiracy sentiments within the general public. This is increasing the chances of a plebiscitary leader rising on a wave populist anti-elitism and leading the general public against the elites. While the fact that government elites are densely networked and influential may be standard for democracy, we do not find it completely normal that most citizens consider elites to be corrupt conspirers isolated in a network of accomplices. Therefore, unwise elite actions are to be warned against. No one can tell if the plebiscitary leader masses might "discover" would be an enlightened democrat, or rather an extremist ready to bury democracy once getting elected.

---

50 Individual and concealed conspiracy against the system one belongs to has a fairly long tradition in the Czech Republic. People demonstrate formal loyalty, and at the same time, informally undermine the authority of the system's institutions. Under the communist regime, people typically behaved differently in public and within the privacy of their homes. While about one-fifth of adults were members of the communist party, the party leadership only exceptionally enjoyed informal respect.

3. To What Extent Is Contemporary Czech Elite Consensual and to What Extent Is It Disunified?

Milan Tuček

3.1 Introduction

We embark on our thinking and analyzing from Field and Higley's (1980) elite development concept, which distinguishes between two types of elites in contemporary meritocratic liberal societies: disunified and consensually unified elites. (A third type, ideologically unified elites, is identified in communist or fundamentalist regimes; their relics or antipodes may be found in post-communist countries as well.) Based on the results of a 2007 empirical study by the CESES team of sociologists, we will attempt to answer the question whether disunity or rather consensual unity (or, as a third option, ideological unity) are characteristic for the current Czech elite in the wake of the third millennium.

In this study, the entire elite has been surveyed, i.e. not only different levels of the political elite but also economic, cultural, media, security, and civic sector elites (see Table 3.1). Our analysis will address the consensus level of the Czech elite as a whole, rather than that of the political elite alone. By all means, the facts under investigation will be difficult to demonstrate. Attitudes and opinions of elite members, studied by means of traditional quantitative survey techniques (standard battery questions with predefined answer scales) are not likely to be absolutely or nearly identical. Furthermore, such a purely mechanical perspective on the facts under investigation may not reveal the level of consensus at all. Therefore, our goal will be to consider opinion differences among individual elite members and, more importantly, between the different elite segments, in the broadest context possible. This will enable us to determine whether specific areas are characterized by opinion agreement, eufunctional differences, or rather more-or-less dysfunctional differences. Obviously, disunity (based on ideology; conflicting political programs; power

Table 3.1: Distribution of respondents among elite segments

		Frequency	Per cent
1	Political: party elites	47	4.5
2	Political: legislative elites	38	3.7
3	Political: local government elites	26	2.5
4	Administrative, executive: ministerial elites	60	5.8
5	Administrative, executive: other	18	1.7
6	Administrative, supervisory: courts and prosecutor's offices	46	4.4
7	Administrative, supervisory: Supreme Audit Office, Office for the Protection of Competition	4	0.4
8	Economic, company sector: domestic capital only	96	9.3
9	Economic, company sector: domestic and foreign capital	111	10.7
10	Economic, company sector: foreign capital only	37	3.6
11	Economic, company sector: financial	16	1.5
12	Media: press elites	71	6.8
13	Media: radio and TV elites	21	2.0
14	Media: advertising and PR agencies	5	0.5
15	Security: police, Ministry of the Interior	34	3.3
16	Security: professional firefighters	17	1.6
17	Security: military elites	26	2.5
18	Cultural: religious elites	24	2.3
19	Cultural: science and education elites	84	8.1
20	Cultural: culture and arts elites	50	4.8
21	Civic: old service elites	60	5.8
22	Civic: old advocacy elites	45	4.3
23	Civic: new service elites	62	6.0
24	Civic: new advocacy elites	17	1.6
25	Civic: infrastructural elites	20	1.9
	Total	1035	99.8*

* Two respondents have not been classified.

struggles; *omnium contra omnes* competition not only in the economy, without respect to macrosocial effects) may and does occur within the different elite segments as well. But a more important problem would exist if membership in different elite segments importantly decreased consensus level across the elite as a whole. That would mean, for instance, that the political and economic elites would compete with each other (political programs and political visions would be in principal conflict with the interests or visions of the economic elites as a whole). Clearly, each elite segment under consideration fulfils a certain function in the social system and has certain interests that are often contradictory to those of other segments. At the same time, different segments may share perceptions and visions of societal development, capacities to seek and find solutions, etc.

It is difficult to determine the extent of sample representativeness for the Czech elite population (in terms of the usual sampling standards). Definitions and mutual proportions of the different segments as well as choice of individuals to represent such segments are subject to discussion. Furthermore, our sampling was influenced by a relatively low response rate. However, we do not doubt that the above segments cover all the important areas of elite activity and our sample of members of these segments makes it possible to map the attitudes and opinions among members of the most important segments of the Czech elite. It is the comparison of attitudes and opinions between these segments that we want to bring forward in our analysis. In order to proceed with analysis, we have created broader segments. We will not only consider opinion differences/homogeneity among those broader segments but also within them. A simple and logical distinction between politicians, high-level officials, members of the economic elite, members of the cultural and media elite, and members of the civic sector elite has been applied (see Table 3.2, which also displays self-declared political orientations on a left-right scale).

Table 3.2: Broader elite segments and their political orientations (per cent)

	Left				Right	Non-response	N
Politicians	23.4	16.2	14.4	21.6	24.3	0.0	111
High-level administrative and security officials	2.0	5.4	35.1	34.6	15.6	6.3	205
Economic elite	0.8	8.8	14.6	35.8	29.2	8.6	260
Cultural and media elite	2.7	11.0	22.7	35.7	20.4	5.9	255
Civic sector elite	10.3	15.2	30.9	26.5	11.8	3.9	204
Total	5.8	10.7	23.9	32.2	20.4	5.7	1035

N.B.: The distribution of left/right political orientations in the Czech general public has been almost constant for the past 8–10 years. In the late 1990s, the distribution on a 7-point scale was as follows: 2% extreme left, 9% left, 13% center-left, 38% center, 18% center-right, 15% right, and 3% extreme right, with 8-10% unable to answer (CVVM 1998). In 2006 (STEM 2006, an extensive representative survey for the Institute of Sociology, Czech Academy of Sciences), the following values were found: 3% extreme left, 9% left, 15% center-left, 42% center, 15% center-right, 13% right, and 3% extreme right. The scale's left/right extremes begin to represent political extremism once the extremes are named (see note on Czech elites' right-wing orientation — neoliberalism — below). Empirical evidence shows that no matter whether the scales have five, seven, nine, ten, or eleven points, whether they are numeric or verbal, and regardless of election results, the left/right political orientation within Czech society have remained steady; the society is not and never was polarized, with most people taking centrist positions and an approximately 10% advantage to the right/center-right orientation.

It must be emphasized that the Czech elite as a whole leans more to the right politically, compared to the general public. However, differences in fundamental political orientations across elite segments are obvious.

An almost symmetrical left/right distribution within the segment of politicians illustrates the well-known fact of left/right power equilibrium in the Czech political scene (in fact, it also represents the will of the electorate, i.e. its political orientations, with the following caveats: the influence of political parties' and individual politicians' image, elections at different levels, election threshold for lower chamber, different election system for the Senate, etc.).

The distribution of political attitudes among civic sector elite members is similar to that among politicians. This is undoubtedly caused by underlying differences in political orientations of civic sector organizations.

The predominant right-wing orientation of the economic elite is hardly surprising. Two-thirds declare this, including one-third with a strong right-wing orientation. Clearly, members of the economic elite tend to associate liberal attitudes and less solidarity/social state with a right-wing political orientation.

For the economic and political elites alike, high percentages at the right margins of the left/right scale should not interpreted as extreme right attitudes, as exemplified by various nationalist or neo-Nazi groups in the Czech Republic, but rather as belief in the above-mentioned liberalism and *laissez-faire* market economy. Those in the left margins of the scale do not favor anarchist movements but rather the Communist Party of Bohemia and Moravia, which identifies with Marxism and aims to change the system (by democratic means). In this respect, the

Communist Party is viewed as a non-system party with zero coalition potential (at least nationally).

Significant for the ways that public discourse, social consciousness, and public opinion are formed is a strong right-wing orientation of the cultural/media elite. Compared to the cultural elite, the media elite is five per cent more "to the right". This situation is undoubtedly a result of the breakdown or discrediting of left-wing concepts, a confused search for a third way, etc. Such political orientation is held by more than just a small number of top-level cultural elite members. College students of both technical and humanities programs (the country's future cultural/technical elite) show similar orientations. The right-wing orientation of the media elite, which has the best chances to influence general public, is based on specific developments within both public and private media organizations back in the first years of transformation (the establishment of TV NOVA in 1994, the so-called Czech TV crisis of 2000/2001, etc.).

The political orientations of Czech administrative and security elites only confirm the important effects of opinion makers and testify the predominant liberal (*laissez-faire*) thought among college-educated professionals beyond public administration.

Table 3.3: "To what extent are you interested in politics?" (Per cent.)

	Very much so	Moderately	Somewhat	Not at all	Non-response	N
Politicians	83.8	13.5	2.7	0.0	0.0	111
High-level administrative and security officials	29.3	53.2	15.6	2.0	0.0	205
Economic elite	14.2	48.1	33.8	3.1	0.8	260
Cultural and media elite	27.1	48.2	22.4	2.0	0.4	255
Civic sector elite	27.0	47.5	22.1	2.0	1.5	204
Total	**30.3**	**45.3**	21.7	2.0	0.6	1035
General population, total (CESES 2008)	4.8	21.3	**47.3**	**25.8**	0.7	2353
College-educated population	10.7	38.5	36.1	14.6	0.0	236

Opinion differences from the political left/right perspective do not necessarily translate into a lack of elite consensus in other opinion areas. The elite is not necessarily torn by opinion conflicts or disunified.

Moreover, the predominant right-wing orientation in most elite segments is a solid foundation for a certain degree of opinion consensus in other areas. Since elite activities often touch the realm of politics, let us outline to what extent these elites declare interest in politics.

The distribution of interest in politics among the different elite segments meets our expectations in that elite — including its economic segment — shows high interest; compared to the general population as a whole, as well as the college-educated portion thereof (see the lowest two rows), even the economic elite clearly interferes with politics, rather than living outside it. The economic elite is little different from college-educated public in the number of those who are not interested in politics. However, no far-reaching conclusions can be derived from the major gap between elite and general public. First, a large portion of members of the above elite segments are directly involved with politics. Second, the public's declared lack of interest in (big) politics does not preclude ordinary people's interest in local affairs, attending parliamentary or local elections, or following the TV news on a daily basis.

3.2 Sources of the Czech Republic's future success

Table 3.4: "Out of the following four areas, chose one that you find most important for the Czech Republic's future success." (Per cent.)

	New industrial technologies	Trust and cohesion among people	Science and research	Citizens' pride and responsibility
Politicians	25.2	15.3	38.7	19.8
High-level administrative and security officials	23.4	15.1	43.4	17.6
Economic elite	39.6	13.8	38.5	7.3
Cultural and media elite	16.5	18.8	43.5	20.4
Civic sector elite	23.0	20.6	32.4	22.5
Total	25.9	16.8	**39.5**	16.9
General population, total (CESES 2008)	25.3	**29.3**	27.2	16.4
College-educated population	25.0	19.1	39.5	16.5

The distribution of answers is similar across all elite segments: two-thirds find science and research the country's most important source of future development (the knowledge society project). Development of new industrial technologies is favored by approximately one-fourth of elite respondents. Trust and cohesion and citizens' responsibility are equally supported by approximately one-eighth. The emphasis by two-fifths of the economic elite on new industrial technologies (at the expense of citizens' responsibility) is the only exception. This hardly surprising deviation in the economic elite's opinions is congruent with its social position and economic role. More surprisingly, the respective roles of other elite segments are not correlated with any other opinion deviations. On the other hand, there were some logical deviations such as stronger emphasis on cohesion and responsibility among members of the civic sector elite and lower emphasis on technologies within the cultural elite.

Notable is the fact that the general public as a whole places most emphasis on trust and cohesion among people. Undoubtedly, this is related to the low prestige of scientific work, insecurity surrounding technological changes, and a traditional idea of a (cohesive) nation-society arising out of Czechs' historic experience.

A certain agreement on the role of science and research as well as other opinions across the elite spectrum might be perceived as a sign of elite consensus on developmental concepts. Compared to the spectrum of opinion within the general public, the indispensable role of elites becomes clear in that the elites are in unavoidable conflict with the conservative thinking of the majority. The fact that the elite's developmental preferences are not even more unambiguous corresponds to its ambiguous feelings about the need of one or several developmental visions (see Table 3.9), i.e. the fact that no single one of these ideas predominated in either elite segment.

3.3 Ratings of the situation in the society

There are no major differences between Czech elite segments in their ratings of the current situation in society. Their satisfaction with the functioning of democracy and state of the economy are high above average (as measured on a 10-point scale). Members of the civic sector elite are more critical in both cases. However, views are vastly divergent within each elite segment, as indicated by standard deviation levels, a fact partially explained by the use of detailed 10-point scales. Not surprisingly, opinions are most differentiated within the political elite, a fact clearly related to each politician's position in the government/opposition struggle. This

Table 3.5: Levels of satisfaction with the functioning of democracy, state of the economy, and the government

	Democracy		Economy		Government	
	Average	Std. dev.	Average	Std. dev.	Average	Std. dev.
Politicians	6.55	2.3	6.60	2.2	4.93	2.9
High-level administrative and security officials	6.93	1.6	6.67	1.8	5.81	1.9
Economic elite	6.42	1.7	6.63	2.0	5.15	2.0
Cultural and media elite	6.34	1.9	6.33	2.0	4.54	1.9
Civic sector elite	6.04	2.0	5.91	2.1	4.46	2.4
Total	6.44	1.9	6.42	2.0	4.97	2.2
General population, total (CESES 2008)	5.20	2.4	4.93	2.3	3.82	2.2
College-educated population	5.83	2.2	5.76	2.3	4.59	2.0

differentiation logically influences government ratings. Satisfaction with the government's functioning is generally slightly below the average and approximately 1.5 points below satisfaction with democracy or economy (even though it is still higher than the general public's satisfaction as measured by repeated opinion polls among adults). Predictably, the media elite and, even more strongly, the cultural elite are more critical than the economic one. Critical ratings by members of the civic sector are also predictable given the level of difficulties their organizations face vis-à-vis public administration. Members of the public administration are the most satisfied with the government (by approximately one point relative to members of other segments). As insiders in this respect, they may be driven by a sense of loyalty to their employer, rather than a critical assessment of the government apparatus's real functioning. And yet another explanation: being insiders, they have sufficient information, as opposed to members of other segments, and therefore, they know the objective limits and possibilities of government functioning.

In summary, the Czech elite is more or less consensual and much less critical in its views of the ways democracy, economy, and even the government are working. However, such a less critical attitude to the real functioning of democracy and economy does not make elites believe that the Czech Republic has reached the standards of modern (Western) societies. Elites are less consensual on the latter point, as demonstrated in the following section.

3.4 The characteristics of contemporary society

The above-mentioned insider position is an important factor of diverging opinions on the characteristics of contemporary society. Opinions tend to converge—both within the elite and between it and general public— on matters that do not directly relate to either elite segment (more than four-fifths agree on social prosperity through debt). When asked a question about "corruption within public administration", 50% of the administrative elite agree, compared to almost 90% of the civic sector elite. As an opposite example, politicians disagree with the media elite in evaluating the "power of the media". Politicians express higher concerns for the mediatization of politics, a situation where the so-called seventh power usurps decision making. The matter is surely more complicated: on one hand, politics and politicians become increasingly vulgar, public opinion is manipulated, etc. and, on the other hand,

Table 3.6: "The Czech Republic has undergone a relatively dramatic development since 1989. Which of the following qualities do you think the country has reached?" (Percentages answering "strongly agree" or "agree", average factor scores.)

	Politicians	Officials	Economic	Cultural	Civic	Total
Open and fair economic competition	56.8	**67.5**	45.7	48.2	**37.6**	49.0
Media have excessive power	**82.9**	72.2	**57.2**	59.9	68.8	64.7
Every citizen's rights and dignity are protected	68.2	**74.0**	57.0	58.3	**51.5**	59.8
Social prosperity through debt	80.0	86.8	88.3	88.4	89.1	85.6
Open and fair competition among political parties	**49.5**	44.6	**21.4**	32.4	**27.2**	32.4
High corruption within public administration	70.9	**51.0**	71.5	83.2	**86.6**	68.0
Factor 1: Fair order	−.33	−.50	.25	.09	.28	
Factor 2: Manipulation, corruption, prosperity through debt	−.17	.01	.19	−.00	−.16	

Factor analysis results (52% of variance)
Factor 1: Open and fair economic competition (.77), Open and fair competition among political parties (.70), Every citizen's rights and dignity are protected (.70), negative High corruption within public administration (-.44)
Factor 2: Media have excessive power (.76), Social prosperity through debt (.63), High corruption within public administration (.52)

the media (journalists) fulfill an indispensable supervisory function, preventing the abuse of power. With 83% answering yes, agreement among politicians goes "across the political spectrum". In contrast, the economic, and cultural/media elites are much more reserved in evaluating the media's power position. They obviously place more emphasis on media's role as the watchdog of democracy and doubt if this function is fulfilled sufficiently and/or brings adequate results (compare with political "insiders" their very low agreement on fair party competition).

Factor analysis has structured the above characteristics of contemporary society into two factors. Factor 1 comprises of key characteristics of social order (modern liberal democracy with emphasis on observing civil rights), while Factor 2 consists of (possible) negative characteristics of the given social order. Factor scores are mathematical constructs calculated for each respondents based on the loadings and values of each answer. Factor scores in the entire sample have normal distribution, average to 0, and have a standard deviation equal to 1. This means that differences greater than 0.5 are statistically significant at a 1% confidence level.

In interpreting the factor analysis results one has to realize that only half of variance has been explained, i.e. the other half of opinion differences is not covered by the above factors. To the explained portion of opinion differences applies that elite segments are almost consensual in (negatively) evaluating social development related characteristics (see average factor scores in Table 3.6). This, however, is not the case with evaluating key characteristics. Differences between average factor scores are significant: on one hand, administration officials and, surprisingly (given the entire political spectrum represented), politicians evaluate contemporary Czech society much more positively than members of the economic and civic sector elites. Percentages indicate that such positive evaluation means that only a slight majority of members of the given segments would find Czech society to be a modern open liberal democracy. In contrast, members of the economic and civic sector elites are predominantly pessimistic. The elite as a whole is consensual insofar as most respondents probably agree on key aspects of a modern democratic society. The fact that elite segments view to what extent these aspects are present in contemporary Czech society differently is clearly related to their respective positions in social life and the (insider/outsider) viewpoints they apply when assessing each aspect.

3.5 Principles of an ideal society

The following text describes findings from a battery of dichotomous questions about principles to be followed by an ideal society. The interpretation of findings should depend on whether the dual principles are really conflicting or rather the fulfillment of one contributes to the fulfillment of the other. The consensual or disunified character of elites

Table 3.7: "What principles should be followed by a society you wish to live in?" (Summed percentages in favor of former statement, average factor scores.)

	Politicians	Officials	Economic	Cultural	Civic	Total
Economic performance v. Easy life	71.7	74.6	**82.2**	*64.3*	*60.2*	68.9
Following traditions v. Modernization changes	40.6	43.5	**22.2**	*36.0*	**28.8**	32.1
Opening up to the world v. Closing up within	76.4	74.1	82.1	82.7	79.4	77.8
Advanced technologies v. Cultural and spiritual development	58.7	57.3	**80.2**	**42.1**	*46.7*	55.7
Creating order v. Maximum freedom	67.7	67.3	66.5	*59.3*	68.3	63.7
Developing talents v. Developing everyone	57.0	69.8	**75.6**	72.0	58.4	66.2
Decentralization, self-help v. Centralization	*71.6*	**85.4**	80.2	80.2	71.7	77.1
Environment v. Economic growth	56.2	65.5	**52.3**	73.6	67.7	81.4
Factor 1: Advanced technologies, performance	.00	−.05	−.35	.20	.25	
Factor 2: Economic growth, modernization	.00	−.14	.35	−.19	−.07	
Factor 3: Open civil society	.18	−.01	−.04	−.16	.19	

Factor analysis results (57% of variance)
Factor 1: Advanced technologies v. Cultural and spiritual development (.70), Developing talents v. Developing everyone (.65), Economic performance v. Easy life (.64), Creating order v. Maximum freedom (.60)
Factor 2: Environment v. Economic growth (.73), Following traditions v. Modernization changes (.68), Creating order v. Maximum freedom (.44)
Factor 3: Decentralization, self-help v. Centralization (.72), Opening up to the world v. Closing up within (.67)

should be interpreted accordingly. Furthermore, the predominant view within each segment needs to be taken into consideration. For most dichotomies, an absolute majority of each segment chose the same option. The choice between advanced technologies versus cultural and spiritual development is the only exception (however, these principles are rather not mutually exclusive), with the economic elite's views in expected sharp contrast to those of the cultural elite.

An overwhelming majority of elite respondents favor opening up to the world, decentralization and self-help in governance, economic performance, and modernization changes. Two-thirds favor creating order, development with respect for the environment, and developing talents first. As a result of the above-mentioned contrast between the economic and cultural elites in their views of advanced technologies versus cultural and spiritual development, overall preferences within the elite as a whole (see the Table's last column) are balanced.

There are important differences between elite segments on some dichotomies. Above all, members of the economic elite strongly prefer modernization (with emphasis on advanced technologies and opening up to the world) along with a performance-oriented society (including a performance-based education system). The other side of the metaphoric barricade is taken by politicians. While an absolute majority of politicians favor the above-mentioned principles as well, their support is much weaker than in the economic elite. We are not sure to what extent this is influenced by diverging political programs (politicians within our sample represent the entire spectrum of left/right orientations, see Table 3.2) with different emphases on each principle, and to what extent it is rather contingent upon individual choice (moderation, less decisiveness, political consideration of alternatives).

Factor analysis has structured those dichotomies into three factors: goal and performance orientation based on advanced technologies; modernization with unlimited economic growth; and an open and decentralized system. This structuring reflects a performance-oriented society with unlimited growth and modern management forms. While those dimensions together represent the ideal of contemporary modern society, factor results surprisingly put them apart. The respective opposite principles that help create the meaning and interpretation of those factors are likely "to blame" here.

The above distribution differences between elite segments are verified in a more concentrated fashion through different average factor scores. The entire left/right political spectrum, as represented by members of the political elite, clearly causes zero factor scores within this segment for both performance and economic growth (like in a "rainbow coalition", competing opinions cancel each other out).

3.6 Broader context of the Czech Republic's development: Orientation on developed Western world

The following questions focus on an area often subject to critical thoughts or debates by important political scientists or sociologists. First, the provincial character of Czech (and generally, most national) elites, and above all, political elites is often debated. Second, numbers of those who view late modernity (contemporary modernization processes) critically are on the rise. Third, the Western Euro-Atlantic civilization's orientation on progress is often not considered ideal. All this is reflected in opinion differences between the different segments of the Czech elite.

Almost 100% of elite members agree that the Czech Republic should raise its economic level to that of the most developed EU countries. This opinion equally predominates in all elite segments and is further confirmed through disagreement with the statement that the country will never catch up with the West. Only a minority of respondents questions the meaning of Western modernization pace, finds the development trajectory predetermined by external factors, or views the chances of Czech society nihilistically. The level of provincialism (or, more positively, patriotic pride) is indicated by the fact that two-thirds believe that Western countries might learn quite a bit from the Czech Republic.

The obligatory factor analysis has structured the battery of questions on the broader context of the Czech Republic's development into two dimensions. The first dimension relates to the (non)questioning of modernization processes. The second refers to contemporary Western society. Within the first dimension, members of the civic sector elite are strongly different from others in questioning the modernization process, while members of the economic elite on the opposite pole have little doubt about the process.

3.7 How to ensure society's future development

Members of the different elite segments are more or less unified in their opinions about whether there is a shared development vision for

Table 3.8: Statements related to the international context of Czech society's development (percentage answering "strongly agree" or "agree", average factor scores)

	Politicians	Officials	Economic	Cultural	Civic	Total
Adaptation to the Western world is inevitable	**48.2**	**67.1**	66.8	57.9	54.8	60.3
The Czech Republic should raise its economic level to that of the most developed EU countries	**99.1**	98.5	95.0	94.9	**88.2**	94.8
Our reproducing Western countries' way of modernization makes no sense	**17.6**	**26.5**	20.3	22.3	26.1	22.9
Western countries' high modernization pace is purposeless	19.5	21.1	20.1	23.6	**36.1**	24.1
While more developed economically, Western countries might learn quite a bit from us	67.6	**72.5**	68.2	**59.8**	69.7	67.5
Ever following the developed West makes no sense, we will never catch up with it anyway	**9.4**	13.9	11.2	12.1	**21.5**	13.8
Spiritual and moral revival is the only way for us to go	29.1	23.5	**17.2**	36.4	**38.8**	28.6
The development of our society has long been predestined by world powers' interests	37.6	**25.2**	33.2	35.7	**52.6**	36.5
Factor 1: Unattainable West, questioning modernization	.07	.08	**.30**	−.08	−.47	
Factor 2: Predetermination of development	.14	.11	−.11	−.03	−.01	

Factor analysis results (56% of variance)
Factor 1: Ever following the developed West makes no sense (.74), Western countries' high modernization pace is purposeless (.73), Our reproducing Western countries' way of modernization makes no sense (.62), The Czech Republic should raise its economic level to that of the most developed EU countries (−.58), Spiritual and moral revival is the only way for us to go (.52), The development of our society has long been predestined by world powers' interests (.52)
Factor 2: Adaptation to the Western world is inevitable (.65), While more developed economically, Western countries might learn quite a bit from us (−.63), The development of our society has long been predestined by world powers' interests (.52)

the Czech Republic, whether there should be just one such vision, who should be the main actor or moving force behind the modernization processes, and what such efforts should be aimed at (see Table 3.9). Partially different are the opinions of economic elites (the role of government, the role of businesspeople in the modernization process, levelling off with the West), which is undoubtedly associated with their liberal views, global economic ties, and practical activities. The fact that civic sector elites are highly skeptical about a shared vision is indicative of their critical views of government policy.

Table 3.9: Statements related to the society's future (percentage answering "strongly agree" or "agree", average factor scores)

	Politicians	Officials	Economic	Cultural	Civic	Total
We are lacking one shared vision	61.8	64.5	**52.4**	66.1	**74.9**	62.2
The government should decide on modernization	**63.0**	54.5	**49.0**	**44.6**	54.5	50.3
Modernization is primarily a matter of individual entrepreneurs	58.3	51.7	**66.5**	56.7	50.0	56.1
We need several visions rather than one vision	53.3	51.8	50.4	53.3	55.1	49.9
We should primarily focus on quickly levelling off with the West	53.8	54.8	**73.1**	51.2	42.4	53.8
People in the Czech Republic are not willing to make sacrifices any more	65.1	60.5	65.5	58.9	60.1	59.9
Factor 1: Liberal decentralization	.10	.06	−.06	−.10	−.00	
Factor 2: Levelling off with the EU	−.05	.13	**−.42**	.20	.23	
Factor 3: Shared vision	.01	-.08	.27	−.06	−.20	

Factor analysis results (62% of variance)
Factor 1: The government should decide on modernization (−.78), Modernization is primarily a matter of individual entrepreneurs (.61), We need several visions rather than one vision (.60)
Factor 2: People in the Czech Republic are not willing to make sacrifices any more (.79), We should primarily focus on quickly levelling off with the West (.67)
Factor 3: We are lacking one shared vision (.90), We should primarily focus on quickly levelling off with the West (−.45)

The structure of ways to ensure and aspects to focus on in the near future is logical. Factor 1 juxtaposes government paternalism with economic subjects taking initiative (as well as the vision of several development trajectories). Factor 2 expresses the belief that levelling off with the West cannot be associated with "belt tightening" any more.

Factor three "separates" the lacking shared vision. Average factor scores for each elite segment demonstrate that there are no marked opinion differences, with the following exception: members of the economic elite clearly stand out in their emphasis on (economic) levelling off with Western countries.

Table 3.10: Statements related to the society's current development (percentage **disagreeing**)

	Politicians	Officials	Economic	Cultural	Civic	Total
Changes in our society are too quick for one to follow	73.6/ **12.7**	75.6/ 18.0	72.2/ **32.9**	71.9/ 22.1	68.8/ 15.8	72.5
Science and technology are the cause of problems rather than their solution	90.0	94.0	86.3	88.8	87.4	89.5
The development of our society is out of our authorities' control	78.7	**81.3**	76.7	75.4	**66.7**	76.4
Further economic growth in our country will not put the environment at risk	59.4	65.3	65.1	**72.3**	**81.1**	71.7
Life in today's society is too complex and unmanageable for a person like me	89.2	**95.1**	91.0	92.1	**82.1**	90.3
Our country is at risk of being taken over by a small group of politicians bribed by big corporations	67.0	73.8	75.1	63.5	54.5	68.5
No one knows where our society is going	73.0	75.4	**78.9**	67.7	**61.6**	72.0
Making decisions about public affairs is too complex for an ordinary person	55.5	57.6	**63.6**	**51.6**	54.0	57.3
Factor 1: Social order anomie	.01	.14	.19	−.14	−.25	
Factor 2: Modern world complexity	.02	.07	−.01	.10	−.24	
Factor 3: Environmental challenge	−.24	−.07	−.01	.02	.20	

N.B.: More pronounced differences between individual elite segments would be found if "strongly disagree" was distinguished from "disagree" (see e.g. the first row, percentages behind slash). As in the other Tables, we focus on the basic yes/no distinction because we find it to sufficient to cover fundamental opinion agreement or disagreement.

Factor analysis results (63% of variance)
Factor 1: No one knows where our society is going (.78), Our country is at risk of being taken over by a small group of politicians bribed by big corporations (.77), Making decisions about public affairs is too complex for an ordinary person (.67), The development of our society is out of our authorities' control (.56)
Factor 2: Science and technology are the cause of problems rather than their solution (.85), Life in today's society is too complex and unmanageable for a person like me (.62), Changes in our society are too quick for one to follow (.57)
Factor 3: Further economic growth in our country will not put the environment at risk (.90)

3.8 How is Czech society developing today?

The last topic focuses on the existence (or perceptions) of various "anomic" aspects in contemporary social development, from mismanaged economic and technological development, to overall regulation of social processes, to feelings of alienation based on little understanding of current social processes. These and similar questions are often asked in public opinion polls. Such polls have repeatedly found high levels of general anomie, shared by all people alike, without differences based on factors like generational identity, education, or other socio-demographic characteristics. These findings raise doubts because society would be facing very serious problems challenging its very essence if the anomie level was so high. We believe that such emotional statements cause frequent stylization and shifts in answers towards greater levels of anomie, and therefore, the functioning of our current social system is not at stake.

First and foremost, the Czech elite's attitudes are realistic in not following the stylization fashions of public opinion. 90% of elite members reject the view that life is too complex and unmanageable for them. Similarly, three-quarters are able to quickly react to changing social environment, do not find society out of control, reject the idea that no one knows where society is going, and do not believe our society might be taken over by political puppets. All this indicates Czech elite members' high self-confidence. Differences between individual segments are rather low and can be traced back to different levels of each segment's engagement in a given subject. Members of the civic elite slightly deviate from this view.

As with the previous battery of questions, opinions are structured in a clear pattern. Factor 1 covers items related to the level of anomie in our social order (note the low perceptions of anomie by elite members). Factor 2 covers perceived (admitted) complexity of the modern world (though elite members understand and know how to act in this world). The last factor separates the environmental challenge, indicating that the topic is perceived differently from anomie or modern world complexities.

3.9 Attempting to evaluate the overall level of consensus in Czech elite: Cluster analysis results

We have tried to use hierarchic cluster analysis to further clarify the ambiguous consensus levels that we found by analyzing answers to the different batteries and, in particular, comparing the percentages

Table 3.11: Hierarchic cluster analysis results: Number and size of opinion-based groups and distribution thereof within elite segments (per cent)

	(A) positive pro-modernization stream	(B) critical stream	(C) conservative stream	(D) left-wing stream
Politicians	45.6	36.8	10.5	7.0
High-level officials	66.0	31.2	2.1	0.7
Economic elite	58.4	38.6	1.2	1.8
Cultural elite	45.7	45.7	6.0	2.6
Civic sector elite	46.4	40.2	7.2	6.2
Total	53.0	38.7	4.4	2.9

Table 3.12: Characteristics of opinion-based groups: Average factor scores (see Legend)

	F11	F12	F41	F42	F43	F71	F72	F101	F102	F103
A	−.35	.40	.02	.06	−.23	.27	.01	.01	−.08	.26
B	.26	−.13	.29	−.06	.11	−.26	−.00	−.09	.11	−.26
C	.10	−.11	−.17	**−.60**	.19	−.02	.41	.57	.61	.21
D	.91	**−.44**	−.32	.39	.50	−.08	**.78**	.17	.00	−.76

	F121	F122	F123	O2_a	O2_b	O2_c
A	.35	−.02	.02	7.63	7.23	6.11
B	−.46	−.08	.06	5.31	5.36	3.82
C	.08	**.60**	−.16	7.07	**8.15**	2.44
D	**−.72**	.12	−.36	2.50	2.83	1.76

Legend:
F11 Order fairness
F12 Manipulation, corruption, prosperity through debt
F41 Advanced technologies, performance
F42 Economic growth, modernization
F43 Open civil society
F71 Unattainable West, questioning modernization
F72 Predetermination of development
F101 Liberal democracy
F102 Levelling off with the EU
F103 Shared vision
F121 Social order anomie
F122 Modern world complexity
F123 Environmental challenge
O2_a Satisfaction with democracy
O2_b Satisfaction with economy
O2_c Satisfaction with government

of agreement/disagreement within individual elite segments. Our goal was to verify whether there are significantly different groups based on opinion distances between elite members, i.e. whether the elite is split by opinions, and if so, whether or not this split goes across individual elite segments. We departed from the results of factor analyses (factor scores), rather than answers to individual questions.

Hierarchic cluster analysis has revealed two large groups that gradually "gathered" over 90% of respondents. While these two groups are, according to characteristics found, strongly different in their opinions to the above issues, they do not constitute bipolarity. More extreme opinions are held by the other two groups which, however, represent as little as 7.3% of respondents (these two do not constitute bipolarity either). Individuals that could not be classified in either group comprise the rest of the sample.

The largest opinion-based group (A) includes more than 50% of elite respondents and has the following characteristics vis-à-vis the second-ranking group (B):

- feeling that today's society is "fair",
- rejecting corruption and prosperity through debt,
- certainty about modernization,
- view that society has one shared vision of future development,
- rejecting the impression of anomie,
- highest satisfaction with democracy, economy, and government functioning.

Group (B) takes opposing views on all the above issues. All aspects show statistically significant differences from the above-discussed average opinions in the elite as a whole (those are normally not neutral). In other words, the group holds above- or under-average opinions. While statistically significant at a 1% confidence level, these differences are not very strong.

In sum, the largest opinion-based group is characterized by viewing positively the achieved level of Czech society's economic transformation, modernization, and democratization. It holds a vision of further development that upholds recent modernization trends as they have occurred in developed Western countries. As for the different elite segments, group (A) has the strongest representation among high-level officials (66%) and also represents an absolute majority of the economic elite (58%).

The second-ranking group (B) represents A's opposite pole (while such polarity is relative, see above). Members of this group critically view the achievements of social transformation, find today's society somewhat dysfunctional, and above all, raise certain doubts about the modernization process/project. They are relatively most frequently represented within the cultural/media elite (45.7%), equaling group A's representation within that segment.

The other groups are rather marginal, although not quite negligible in terms of representation among politicians and the civic sector elite. The larger of these, group C, is characterized by high satisfaction with the economy on one hand, and conservative views of modernization and economic growth on the other. Group D is extremely dissatisfied with the social situation, reserved towards social order, and doubtful about the fairness of political and economic competition. We can assume that conservative politicians belong to the former group and extreme left-wing politicians to the latter.

3.10 Conclusion

As stated in the introduction, the question of elite consensus is a key one. Without doubt, elites — here primarily individual elite segments — that are mostly consensual in their views of the state and development of the society and strategies for the future (provided they normally communicate in order to make consensus a possibility), fulfill the necessary integration role both within the nation and externally, in its integration efforts within European and global structures. To sum up, contemporary Czech elite as represented by the above study shows a high level of consensus in all substantial areas and issues under investigation. This consensus is clearly based on the predominant liberal thinking among elite respondents, their pro-modernization orientation, and refusal to close up within national boundaries. However, such (positive) findings may be contingent upon the economic and overall social situation at the time of data collection (late 2007). The results might be different now that the national economy is in recession and the country is headed towards an early election. While we do not assume that elite members' predominant ideological orientations would change substantially, the upcoming power struggle will necessarily stage more pronounced articulations of those issues that differentiate Czech elites. Last but not least, this power struggle will depend on getting as much public support as possible, and therefore, a rational strategy for elites to obtain power positions might be to somewhat shift their opinions closer to public opinion — one we demonstrated is on many issues different from that of elite members.

4. Values of the Elite and the General Public as Sources of Cohesion

Libor Prudký

4.1 Values and social cohesion: Mutual links and influences

One may come across numerous concepts of values in literature.[51] No matter how values are defined, they are practically always linked to social cohesion, either explicitly (recently in the Czech Republic as one of the major themes of Jiří Musil's study on social and cultural cohesion, 2004) or implicitly (e.g. in de Moor's analyses of the European Values Study results, 1995). This is because values are always viewed as something important for specifying the essence of every social object, including its motivation, behavior, culture, reflection, and self-reflection. Values are unavoidable when analyzing the reasons why a given social object holds together.

The mere fact that the level of shared values is related to social cohesion is less important than the quality of such relationship. Answers to this question vary. Some sources, and in particular Parson's social systems theory, view values as one of the society's cornerstones; the level of value sharing determines the very existence of society. Authors of another extreme view values as a multidimensional concept with multiple meanings, and therefore, reject the presumably misleading study of values. Contemporary sociologists often approach values as a concept as diversified as society itself. Parson's perspective of "minimum shared values" as a precondition for the existence of society is obsolete for the study of values in a post-modern society, e.g. based on a Foucauldian approach. Rather than sources of sharing, consensus, and equilibrium, values are studied as attributes of differentiation, diversification, struggles, or even breakdown. However, the threat of anomie makes

---

51 Hofstede discusses over 900 concepts, merely based on resources that existed within American sociology before the end of the 1970s.

investigation of the nature, importance, and place of values in social order essential. Therefore, values come back to us at different levels and in different contexts, even when we analyze contemporary society based on different postmodern concepts.

More and more markedly emerges the issue of values in relation to the developing knowledge of social structure. The traditional status characteristics are strongly influenced by lifestyle and life culture. We see growing and changing perspectives and levels that determine and dynamize the status of individuals, groups, and strata within society. They are influenced by aspects of different cultures and ethnicities. The external conditions of socialization (with values as one of the essential building blocks of personality development) are increasingly dynamic, including new mediators, and all this — along with numerous other influences — restructures and constantly changes society. These processes also naturally affect the relationship between elites and the general public, including their internal differentiation and the dynamic of change.

The study of new forms of social structure is essential for us to find answers to numerous questions, including that of the nature of social cohesion. Under these circumstances, doubts are often expressed over major empirical social surveys of values. Such doubts are legitimate for the following reason: while all these great conceptions of international empirical studies of value structures are culturally embedded in certain civilization assumptions, they are being implanted into cultures that do not correspond with such assumptions. In spite of that, large international sociological surveys of value structures continue to be carried out.[52] We will treat such surveys as a mere basic framework for further analysis. Hard conclusions about differences between cultures or civilizations such as those offered by Inglehart's "maps of materialist/ postmaterialist societies" are considered illustrations rather than findings. This is not only a result of the fact that the instruments applied to specify such societies are extremely rough and their correlation with alternative approaches to investigating values is rarely analyzed.[53] On the other hand, the findings of representative social surveys that address and investigate values as a mass phenomenon cannot be ignored when looking at the value structure of any given society.

---

52 Most recently, the European Values Study was carried out in 2008. Results were not available by the time the present text was submitted.

53 In order to contribute to developing empirical instruments of the sociological study of value structures, one of the partial goals of this analysis is to show a possible correlation between Inglehart's and some other approaches to the study of values.

In the present study we work with the results of quantitative empirical social surveys that were carried out among the general adult population of the Czech Republic as well as the country's functionally defined elites. In this way, we identify the basic outlines of the value structures of the Czech Republic's elites and general adult population as one general way to explain the level of cohesion within elites and society as a whole. Our fundamental assumption is that the extent of similarity (convergence) of the value structures adopted by elites and society as a whole, respectively, may facilitate social cohesion within the Czech Republic's society. Therefore, our analysis aims to describe this convergence (or divergence) and its development throughout recent years.

In order to study the function of values in social cohesion, we will first need to describe our working concept of values.

Two concepts of values were applied in the empirical surveys that we analyze. Rokeach's (1972) concept — which in some aspects builds on Parsons (1951) and Kluckhohn (1947) — created a new foundation for using empirical surveys to study values. For this purpose, two types of values are distinguished: terminal and instrumental. The former type is understood as something that ought to be (as an end), the latter as something that is (as accepted by society or its parts to be substantial for life, decision making, motivation, and behavior because it is accepted as part of the defined contents of social phenomena and processes).

Rokeach's concept was most markedly developed by R. Inglehart (1977, 1993). His famous theory of materialist/postmaterialist values is often applied, in spite of all criticism. Inglehart's core battery of questions was also applied in our three surveys. We understand this as a departure point for our understanding of terminal values, given the wording of the questions that inquire respondents directly about the given country's future and orientation of development.

In order to identify the basic characteristics of values as something that exists, something that may or may not be shared within society and, as such, may to differing degrees become a source of social cohesion, we have adapted the batteries on value structures from large international empirical value surveys, and in particular, the European Values Study. Those batteries have been developed and verified by the CESES team with a long-term perspective.[54]

---

54 Part of a National Research Program project on the relationship between value structures and stratification that has been carried out by members of the CESES and the Institute of Sociology, Czech Academy of Sciences. The author of this text is the project's principal investigator.

The dual perspective makes it possible not only to view value structures from different angles, but also to verify the above assumptions by looking at mutual relationships. This represents one of the important methodological goals of our analysis. The application of Inglehart's macro approach to groups like elites is compared to the application of the approach our team developed to analyze value structures. The types of materialist/postmaterialist value supporters are compared with a more detailed typology which is based on value orientations and specifies etatists, liberals, egalitarians, conformists, xenophobes, and partially hedonists, individualists, and religious values supporters. The possibilities for complementarity between both approaches are among the basic conceptual questions leading our analysis.

We will attempt to clarify both dimensions of values and the relationships between them among Czech elites (as a whole and within individual elite segments) and the general public, looking into the level of convergence/divergence. We will do so by looking at frequencies and characterizing the supporters of different terminal values and existing value structures. Then we will attempt to specify the level of value convergence according to both Inglehart and the more general concept, among elites and the general public. Such convergence will be understood as a possible departure point for further analyzing the sources of social cohesion within the Czech society.

From the perspective of governance, the main question is to what extent this country enjoys value convergence between elite and the general public as a precondition for effective governance.

Further analyses will build on data from the 2004 survey of elites and the 2003 survey of the general population as both make direct comparison of data on values according to Inglehart's and our approaches possible. Data from other surveys presented here (Elites 2007, General population 2005, General population 2008) will be primarily used to describe the dynamic of development and change in Czech elite and general public's value structures over time.

4.2 Materialist and postmaterialist values in Czech elites and general public

Results of the 1991 and 1999 European Value Studies as well as our own survey of 2005 demonstrate the predominance of materialist value orientations, according to Inglehart. However, the index[55] has grown from negative 26 percentage points (in favor of materialist values) in 1991 to negative 15 points in both 1999 and 2005. This shift might mean the growing importance of postmaterialist values (postmaterialization) or declining importance of materialist values (dematerialization). Both processes seem to have occurred simultaneously. The proportion of postmaterialist respondents has grown by more than a half (from 6% to over 9%) even if it continues to be substantially lower than that of materialists. Most people have consistently belonged to the mixed type. In conclusion, Inglehart's central thesis on growing postmaterialist tendencies in contemporary societies seems to be valid in Czech society, while the materialist orientation continues to strongly predominate.

In international comparison, the 1999 results for the Czech Republic are close to those of Finland, Germany, and Iceland. Distance from other post-communist countries has grown markedly, while the country's level continues to be far below that of the Netherlands and Nordic countries.

Table 4.1: Distribution of answers to the dual question "What should our country's goals be for the next ten or fifteen years" that is central to Inglehart's typology of value orientations (per cent)

Answer options	Elites 2004		General Population 2003		General Population 2008	
	1st choice	2nd choice	1st choice	2nd choice	1st choice	2nd choice
(a) Maintaining order	36.5	28.1	49.3	24.7	34.2	30.3
(b) Giving people more say in important decisions	27.3	29.9	28.7	27.5	27.6	23.8
(c) Fighting rising prices	2.8	9.9	13.7	26.8	27.6	28.6
(d) Protecting freedom of speech	33.5	32.1	8.4	21.0	8.9	15.0

---

55 Value orientation types are constructed from answers to repeated four-item questions. Options (a) "Maintaining order" and (c) "Fighting rising prices" express a materialist orientation, while options (b) "Giving people more say" and (d) "Protecting freedom of speech" stand for postmaterialist values. In Inglehart's approach, the repeated question is "what should this country's goals be for the next ten or fifteen years". Respondents are first asked to choose a top-priority goal and then their "second choice". Those who choose materialist values in both rounds are classified as the materialist type, those with two postmaterialist choices are classified postmaterialists. Those who choose values of different types in the two rounds fall into a "mixed" category. The index is calculated by subtracting the proportion of postmaterialists from that of materialists.

In order to describe these processes, it is essential to find out who the supporters of the different Inglehartian value orientations are. Inglehart (1997: 134) assumed that the rich, educated, and young should support postmaterialist values, and used international data to demonstrate the relationship between value orientations and age, education attainment, and income.

As a first step in our analysis, we will compare elites and the general population based on Inglehart's approach to value orientations.

The resulting distribution of types becomes apparent in the following Figure.

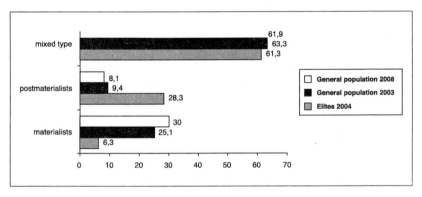

Figure 4.1: Distribution of Inglehartian value orientation types among Czech elites and general population (per cent)

Using the standard Inglehartian approach to summary analysis, we have determined the following marked differences:

- postmaterialists are more numerous than materialists among elites. The index value (+22 points) is strongly in favor of postmaterialists,
- materialists predominate over postmaterialists in the general population. Index values of −17 points in 2003 and −20.6 (2008) demonstrate a slight increase of materialist value orientations in the Czech Republic's general population over the past five years,
- the mixed value type, the least defined one according to Inglehart, continues to be the most predominant in the Czech Republic's elites as well as general population.

Elite value orientations are clearly differentiated across the different elite segments.

Table 4.2: Distribution of Inglehartian value orientation types among elite segments (2004)

Elite segment	Materialists (per cent)	Postmaterialists (per cent)	Index	Mixed type (per cent)
Political	4.5	32.6	+28.1	62.9
Economic	10.8	17.3	+6.5	71.9
Administrative	8.2	23.5	+15.3	57.7
Media	5.4	36.9	+31.5	68.2
Other (science, culture, education, arts, religious): traditional cultural elites	4.4	35.5	+31.1	60.1

The postmaterialist orientation is more frequently supported by elite members from the media, traditional cultural elites, and political elites. In contrast, the economic and administrative elites are characterized by smaller predominance of postmaterialist value orientations over materialist ones.

Differences are independent of gender and education (after all, Czech elites are strongly homogenous in terms of education, embracing very few people with less than full secondary education). Age is insignificant in elites but it is of influence in the general population. This confirms Inglehart's assumption that postmaterialists are more frequent in the younger age categories. Notably, postmaterialist elite members include substantially higher numbers of respondents with declared religiosity based on regular churchgoing — a rather traditional form of religiosity. No declared faith, or faith without religious affiliation (considered a modern form of religiosity), are more characteristic of materialists.

Both general population surveys confirmed that postmaterialists are younger and more educated. Furthermore, materialists are more frequently found in lower income categories, smaller municipalities, and among married respondents. Men are more likely to be postmaterialist, while women more frequently support the materialist value orientation. These findings basically confirm Inglehart's assumptions about the supporters of postmaterialist values.

4.3 The structure of existing values among Czech elites and general population

The second approach to the study of elite and general public values is based on investigating certain attributes of value structures. As mentioned above, we assume that these are adopted value structures in the form of existing sources of motivation, experience, identification of self and community, and behavior, rather than terminal values.

Our first question is: what is the nature of any differences in existing values between elites and the general population? Second, we want to know whether and how elites themselves are differentiated in this respect.

Once again, we will attempt to answer these questions by analyzing the level of elite-public convergence in terms of life values and value orientations, including their different supporters. Following this we will specify the nature of value structures in individual elite segments.

We compare life values by analyzing the ways respondents assign weights to six different values in life.

Table 4.3: Comparing the weights of life values in the Czech Republic (as average scores on a 4-point scale, 1 = maximum weight, data from Elites 2004 and General population 2003)

Dataset	Work	Family	Friends	Leisure	Politics	Religion
Elites 2004	1.23	1.13	1.58	2.09	2.36	3.07
General population 2003	1.61	1.21	1.68	1.58	3.08	3.33

There are clear differences between elites and the general population for the values of work, leisure, politics, and religion. Differences are high between value structures, rather than individual values separately. Leisure is much more important to the Czech Republic's general adult population than it is for its elites. In contrast, work and religion are very important to elites.

Once again, elites are not entirely homogenous here. The different elite segments place different emphases on the values of politics (found important by about one-third of economic elites and almost 85% of political elites); religion (important to 80% of "other" elites, but only 10% of economic elites); and leisure (important to 80% of media elites as opposed to just 65% of political elites). Economic elites are the closest to the general population in their life value structures, while cultural elites are the most distant.

Life values are highly resistant to change and tend to show minimum differences. Any difference demonstrated therefore represents an important finding. However, the measures used are rather rough, with questionable distinctive potential. The ranking of life values says little about their contents. Any convergence/divergence in value orientations is more important for specifying content and direction. We have been able to compare the Czech 2004 elites with the 2003 general population on five types of value orientations.

Table 4.4: Comparing selected value orientations among the Czech Republic's elite and general population (average scores, on a 4-point scale from 1=strongly agree to 4=strongly disagree, and percentages of consent)

Value orientation type as consent with the statement presented	Elites 2004		General population 2003	
	Average score	Consent (per cent)	Average score	Consent (per cent)
People's problems should be primarily addressed by the state, rather than by people (etatist)	3.09	19.3	2.68	52.2
Security and wealth are more important than freedom (non-liberal)	3.45	8.9	3.10	31.1
Foreigners should be banned from all political activities in our country (xenophobic)	3.23	17.5	2.82	54.3
Income differences should decrease (egalitarian)	3.01	26.4	2.08	77.0
One best lives peacefully and stays in line with others in order to avoid unnecessary trouble (conformist)	3.51	7.6	2.77	50.8

There are marked differences between elites and the general population in all types of value orientations. The general adult population tends to agree with each statement more often than elites and, in some instances, the two groups hold opposing attitudes. The general adult population has a clear majority of egalitarians over proponents of differentiation; etatists predominate over their counterparts; people with xenophobic orientations are more numerous than those open to foreigners and diversity; and the conformist orientation prevails over orientation on exceptionality. Elites lean towards the opposite poles on all four of these scales. Moreover, the predominance of liberals is markedly stronger in elites than in the general adult population.

The above differences are deeper in cultural elites, while economic elites are the closest to the general population. This, however, does not apply to egalitarian and xenophobic orientations, on which all elite segments show similar attitudes that are markedly different from those of the general population.

These findings go along with the above evidence on value distances between elites and the general population as well as distances between individual elite segments (and between parts of the general population). Undoubtedly, those entities are not value homogenous.

4.4 Comparing Inglehartian value types with value orientation types

Comparing value types according to Inglehart with types of value orientations may clarify both our analysis of internal value structures in elites and the general public and our comparison of convergence/ divergence. This comparison is based on analyzing pair relationships between indicators of the different approaches to studying values and analyzing the characteristics of the different value orientation supporters. Once again, our data comes from the 2004 elite survey and the 2003 general adult population survey. (more recent data do not allow for such comparison) Clearly, we have been able to compare variables that were included in both surveys only.

We have demonstrated a pattern of relationship between Inglehartian value types and value orientation types. While materialists coincide with the etatist, non-liberal, xenophobic, egalitarian, and conformist elite members, postmaterialists tend to be non-etatist, liberal, open to foreigners and diversity, in favor of differentiation, and non-conformist. This pattern of relationship emerges from mutual comparisons as well as supporter characteristics. 10 out of 11 total compatible characteristics that are statistically significantly correlated with the Inglehartian materialist value type are also correlated with our value orientation types. The strongest associations exist between materialist elite members and their etatist, non-liberal, xenophobic, egalitarian, and conformist orientations, generalized mistrust, reluctance to acknowledge moral commitment for holding their own elite functions, and rejection of religiosity. This pattern of relationship might indeed be subject to serious doubt if it did not similarly exist in the general population as well.

As in the general adult population of the Czech Republic, materialists tend to display etatist, non-liberal, xenophobic, egalitarian, and conformist orientations. In contrast, postmaterialists tend to oppose etatism, be liberal and open to foreigners and diversity, and favor differentiation and exceptionality. Recall that the relative proportion of postmaterialists versus materialists among elite respondents is the reverse of that in the general population. Despite this, both approaches to studying values yield similar results.

Table 4.5: Characterizing supporters of the different Inglehartian values and value orientation types, Elites 2004, Czech Republic

Indicator	Inglehartian		Value orientations				
	Materialist	Postmaterialist	Etatist	Non-liberal	Xenophobic	Egalitarian	Conformist
Gender	–	–	–	–	Women	–	–
Education	–	–	Vocational training, secondary	–	Secondary, vocational training	Secondary, vocational training	–
Age	–	–	–	–	–	–	Older
Profession	Local administration	Media	Firms, administration	Administration, firms	–	–	–
PC with internet	Disagree	Agree	–	Disagree	Disagree	Disagree	–
Elite segments	economic, administrative	cultural, media	economic	economic	–	–	economic, administrative
Generalized trust	No	Yes	No	No	No	No	Little
Elite-public tension	Agree	Disagree	Rather agree	Rather agree	Rather agree	Rather agree	–
Interest in politics	Little	High	Rather disagree	Rather disagree	Rather disagree	–	Rather disagree
Religiosity	Not practicing religious, non-religious	Practicing religious	Atheist	Atheist, non-religious	–	–	–
Elites' moral commitment	Disagree	Agree	Disagree	Disagree	Disagree	–	Disagree
Work value	Rather disagree	Rather agree	Rather disagree	Rather disagree	–	Rather disagree	–
Family value	–	–	–	–	–	–	–
Friends value	–	–	–	–	–	–	–
Leisure value	–	–	–	–	–	Not important	–
Politics value	Rather disagree	Rather agree	Rather disagree	Rather disagree	Disagree	–	Rather disagree
Religion value	Rather disagree,	Agree	Rather disagree	Disagree	Rather disagree	Disagree	Rather disagree
Etatist	Rather agree	Disagree					
Non-liberal	Rather agree, Rather disagree	Disagree	x	x	x	x	x
Xenophobic	Rather agree	Disagree	x	x	x	x	x
Egalitarian	Rather agree	Disagree	x	x	x	x	x
Conformist	Rather agree	Disagree	x	x	x	x	x

Note: Statistically significant relationships are indicated explicitly; dash ("–") indicates cells with no significant relationships; meaningless relationships are crossed out ("x").

Table 4.6: Characterizing supporters of the different Inglehartian values and value orientation types, General adult population 2003, Czech Republic

Indicator	Inglehartian		Value orientations				
	Materialist	Postmaterialist	Etatist	Non-liberal	Xenophobic	Egalitarian	Conformist
Gender	Women	Men	Women	–	Men	Women	Women
Education	Vocational training, primary	Secondary, tertiary, primary	Primary	Vocational training, primary	Vocational training	Primary	Primary
Age	Older	Younger	Older	Older	Older	Rather older	Older
Income	Lower	Higher	Lower	Lower	Lower	Lower	Lower
PC with internet	No	Yes	No	No	No	No	No
City/ countryside	Countryside	Rather city	Countryside	Countryside	Countryside	Countryside	Countryside
Region (old)*	M	Prague, EB	EB, SB, Prague	CB, NB, NM	SM, SB, NM	NM, SM (NB)	NB, NM
Generalized trust	No	Yes	–	No	No	No	No
General satisfaction	Rather low	High	Low	Low	Low	Low	Low
Religiosity	Practicing	Religious without affiliation, Non-religious	Practicing	Non--religious, atheist	Atheist	Practicing	Practicing
Work value	Rather disagree, Disagree	Agree	Rather agree	Rather agree	Rather agree	Rather agree	Rather disagree
Family value	–	–	Rather agree	Rather disagree	Rather agree	Rather agree	Rather disagree
Friends value	Rather agree	Strongly agree	Rather disagree	Disagree	Disagree	Rather disagree	Disagree
Leisure value	Rather agree	Strongly agree	Rather disagree	Rather disagree	Rather agree	Rather agree	Disagree
Politics value	Strongly disagree	Rather agree	Rather disagree	Disagree	Rather disagree	Disagree	Strongly disagree
Religion value	–	–	Rather agree	Rather disagree	Disagree	Rather disagree	Agree
Etatist	Agree	Disagree	x	x	x	x	x
Non-liberal	Agree	Disagree	x	x	x	x	x
Xenophobic	Agree	Disagree	x	x	x	x	x
Egalitarian	Agree	Disagree	x	x	x	x	x
Conformist	Agree	Disagree	x	x	x	x	x

Note: Statistically significant relationships are indicated explicitly; dash ("–") indicates cells with no significant relationships; meaningless relationships are crossed out ("x").
* Regions of residence are classified in line with the system in place before 2000: B = Bohemia, M = Moravia, N = North, S = South, E = East, W = West, C = Central.

Similarly to elites, 12 out of 15 total compatible characteristics that are statistically significantly correlated with the Inglehartian materialist value type are also correlated with our value orientation types. (Conversely, supporters of postmaterialist values tend to be open, liberal, non-conformist, in favor of differentiation, and opposed to etatism.) A strong association between the postmaterialist type and general life satisfaction is notable: postmaterialist values seem to be associated with factors facilitating such satisfaction, while materialist values tend to have the opposite effect. At the same time, higher general life satisfaction is associated with greater openness, non-conformity, differentiation, not relying on government aid, and liberalism.

In this respect, there is a strong agreement between elites and the general population, yet with reverse proportions: the high proportion of postmaterialists among elites is similar to the low proportion of postmaterialists within the general adult population.

Simultaneously, the economic segment and, to a lower degree, the administrative segment stand out among elites, should we apply Ingelhart's typology, by being more materialist. Conversely, cultural elites (also referred to as "other", i.e. artists, scientists, academic scholars, religious leaders, etc.) and media elites show higher support for postmaterialist values. Political elites are in between, perhaps closer to the postmaterialist type, and therefore more open, liberal, non-etatist, non-conformist, and favoring differentiation.

Based on the above results of comparison between both approaches to analyzing values in the Czech Republic's elites and general adult population, we choose to continue to apply the value orientation types in our further analyzing value structures as possible sources of cohesion. We will treat value orientation types in their own name and also as representatives of the Inglehartian value types. Therefore, a more general hypothesis follows: the Inglehartian value typology embraces more detailed value orientation types. Accordingly, we can infer Inglehartian value types based on the strength of association thereof with individual value orientation types.

4.5 Recent developments of value orientation types in the Czech Republic's elites and general public

We will apply five types of value orientations in order to grasp developments of the Czech elites and general population values over time. Each predominant orientation will be compared with its less-represented counterpart.

Table 4.7: Relative predominance of selected value orientation types in Czech elites (percentage points)

Predominant value orientation	Distance (2004)	Distance (2007)
– non-etatist over etatist	+60.6	+34.8
– liberal over non-liberal	+81.5	+77.3
– open over xenophobic	+64.6	+58.6
– differentiating over egalitarian	+47.0	+28.8
– nonconformist over conformist	+84.4	+63.0

Shifts over time may be a result of specific developments (e.g. growth of egalitarian tendencies may be associated with the growing actual income differentiation in society) as well as diminishing differentiation within elites. While elites continue to be predominantly oriented towards an open society, the general trend is towards less openness.

Shifts in predominant value types between 2003, 2005, and 2008 may be observed in the general adult population.

Table 4.8: Relative predominance of selected value orientation types in the Czech general adult population (percentage points)

Predominant value orientation	Distance (2003)	Distance (2005)	Distance (2008)
– etatist over non-etatist	+10.3	+8.0	+14.1
– liberal over non-liberal	+31.2	+23.7	+31.2
– xenophobic over open	+18.6	+20.7	+12.2
– egalitarian over differentiating	+57.6	+59.4	+51.9
– conformist over nonconformist	+7.4	+31.1	+16.9

Several clear findings arise out of the above comparison:

- there are substantial differences between the value orientations of the Czech Republic's elites and general public (population) in terms of etatism, xenophobia, egalitarianism, and conformity. Elite orientations are in fact the reverse of those of the general public,
- these differences do not change dramatically over time. The predominance of the different value orientation types in elites diminishes over time, and thus, elites are drawing slightly closer to the general public;

- liberal orientations prevail in the general public as well as elites, but the distance in elites is more than double the size. However, the general orientation is the same for both elites and the general public.

The above comparisons reveal that no value convergence between elites and the general public is available to facilitate social cohesion between elites and the general population.

Since 2005, we have investigated other types of value orientations in surveys as well. Elite-public differences on these new measures are less significant than those demonstrated in the above analysis. Both elites and the general public prefer hedonistic values over moderation, individualism over cooperation, and values related to non-religious orientations over pro-religious values. Except for the latter orientation, differences are rather low. These comparisons are more promising for facilitating social cohesion between elites and the general population.

4.5 Possible conclusions

Findings of the analysis presented above can be summarized in several ways. Comparing Inglehart's approach to studying values with another approach has contributed methodologically: we have learned that the two approaches can be compared and interpreted from two perspectives. First, while the Inglehartian approach rather focuses on terminal values and ours on instrumental values, there is a strong relationship between both types of values. Second, Inglehart's general materialist/postmaterialist distinction of value structures can be viewed as embracing (summarizing) predominant values; a new approach to studying values can specify this general typology in more detail.

Material findings will be summarized from the perspective of our belief that the level of convergence in value structures is one of the foundations of social cohesion, while value divergence impedes efforts for stronger cohesion in society or parts thereof. First, evidence of the Czech elites' internal cohesion shows (based on both approaches to studying values) three distinct groups among the elites. One pole is occupied by members of the economic elite along with the administrative elite, characterized by a strong materialist orientation, growing etatist orientation, conformism, and non-liberal values. The opposite pole is represented by members of the cultural and media elites, with clear orientations on values facilitating open society. Political elites are between these two poles. The level of cohesion within elites is rather low. While convergence of value orientations grows, the elite remains separated into the three groups. This can be interpreted as evidence of the fact that elites themselves have difficulties acting as one cohesive body, and therefore, their actions and roles as reference groups can hardly facilitate the growth of social cohesion in Czech society. Their value influence is in fact ambiguous: while the economic and administrative elites work towards closed society, the cultural and media elites can be expected to strive for an open society.

Differences between elites and the general population are even more pronounced than those within elites. The Inglehartian mixed type is the most frequent among elites as well as the general population. This fact might seem to be a possible source of growing social cohesion. However, the mixed type is characterized by ambiguity, and cannot be specified based on Inglehart's typology. In contrast, our approach to studying value preferences and types of value orientations shows that mixed type respondents in the general public support different value orientations than mixed type elite respondents, especially those of the culture/media elite as well as the political elite. The economic and administrative elites are closer to the general population. On the other hand, younger, college-educated, and highly qualified or creative profession oriented members of the general population are closer to the cultural and media elites.

The comparison reveals that predominant value orientations (terminal and instrumental alike) in the Czech Republic's general population have been different from those in its elites over the recent years. While elites tend to support values facilitating open society, the general public rather supports closed society and upholding existing order. This is yet another dimension jeopardizing social cohesion in the country.

5. Elites, General Public, and Democracy

Martin Nekola

5.1 Introduction

It has been twenty years since the November 1989 revolutionary events launched the process of democratization in the former Czechoslovakia and, from 1993, the Czech Republic. During that time, political scientists have paid major attention to democratic transition (see Dvořáková & Kunc 1994), and later the gradual consolidation of democracy into a more-or-less specific form of post-socialist political regime. At the end of 21st century's first decade, Czech democracy is considered consolidated and relatively mature, which brings new problems and risks as we know from developed Western European democracies. These include, above all, falling citizen trust in politicians and political institutions as well as decreasing electoral participation, a fact some authors find to be a symptom of the so-called crisis of democracy (see Crozier, Huntington & Watanuki 1975; Huntington 1981) or political isolation (Putnam 1995). This development has hardly been affected by the "victory of democracy" over communism (Huntington 1991; Fukuyama 1992). Ever growing numbers of analyses and international comparative studies demonstrate diminishing support for politics in the United States (see Nye 1997) as well as Western European countries (see e.g. Dalton 1996; Klingemann & Fuchs 1995).

The situation in post-communist countries is somewhat more complicated, relative to Western Europe, given the social transitions that occurred in early 1990s and the subsequent transformation of political, economic, and social systems. The Czech Republic experienced a strong transformation ethos during this time period, resulting in high trust in political representatives and the democratic regime along with high voter turnout. However, in recent years, the country has experienced a rapid decline in trust as well as electoral participation, giving rise to serious doubts about the stability of new democracies and warnings of a return to undemocratic forms of governance.

In the following chapter, we will focus on studying democracy as a form of political regime and power sharing between elites and the general public. We depart from the well-known thesis that citizen (Easton 1975, 1979) and elite (Eldersveld 1989, Remmer 1991, Diamond 1999) support is essential to a political system's viability. The elite-public relationship is seen from the perspective of both parts' respective roles in the democratic political system and real effects of their actions on the system. Based on the concept of political support, we will seek answers to the following questions:

(1) What form of political regime is supported by the Czech Republic's general public and its elites?

(2) How is the current political regime evaluated by the general public and elites?

(3) To what extent do the general public and elites fulfill mutual expectations?

We will analyze data from two quantitative surveys by the CESES among Czech elites (2007) and general public (2008) that are described in the introduction to this book.

Analysis will focus on two basic levels of comparison: first, the elite-public comparison, and second, differences within both groups of actors, i.e. among individual elite and public categories respectively. We assume key differentiation within elites based on elite segmentation (political, administrative, economic, media, security, cultural, and civic elites) and party preferences (the party chosen by respondent in the most recent lower chamber election). Differentiation within the general public will be studied based on individual respondents' party preferences[56] and socio-economic status.[57] As for the latter factor, we have split the general public into four status quartiles according to the International Socio-economic Index of Occupational Status (further referred to as ISEI), from the lowest to the highest quartile.

In our elite-public comparison, we want to know what democracy-related attitudes elites and the general public agree on and, in contrast, what topics are subject to conflicting views. At the same

---

56 As measured by the question, "Who would you vote for if the Chamber of Deputies election took place next week?"

57 We have applied the International Socio-economic Index of Occupational Status created by Ganzeboom, De Graaf & Treiman (1992).

time, we attempt to answer a question that arose at the beginning of our research effort several years ago when we defined elites as people holding important positions (see the above summary description of this study): aren't elites, based on this definition, merely a part of the general public that is more educated and holds more prestigious or better paid jobs? Thus, can any elite-public differences be explained merely based on education level or socio-economic status, rather than elite membership? In other words, can elite status play any role at all and do elites share attitudes that are different from non-elites with the highest socio-economic status?

Table 5.1: Distribution of variables differentiating within elites and the general public

Elites 2007				General Public 2008		
Elite segment	**Frequency**	**Percent**		**ISEI quartiles**	**Frequency**	**Percent**
Political	111	11		First	402	17
Administrative	128	12		Second	586	25
Economic	260	25		Third	444	19
Media	97	9		Fourth	626	27
Security	77	7		Missing	295	13
Cultural	158	15		Total	2353	100
Civic	204	20				
Total	1035	100				
Party (last elections)	**Frequency**	**Percent**		**Party (elections next week)**	**Frequency**	**Percent**
ODS	383	37		ODS	366	16
ČSSD	162	16		ČSSD	541	23
KDU-ČSL	88	9		KDU-ČSL	150	6
KSČM	37	4		KSČM	211	9
Greens	84	8		Greens	104	4
Other party	54	5		Other party	183	8
No vote	69	7		Would not vote	404	17
Do not know	10	1		Do not know	283	12
Non-response	148	14		Non-response	111	5
Total	1035	100		Total	2353	100

Sources: CESES 2007, 2008

In the latter comparison, we are offering a more detailed look "inside" both groups, focusing on convergent/divergent democracy-related attitudes between the different elite segments and status groups. In this sense, we understand democracy as an institutional regime of power relations between elites and the general public in which political parties play an important part. Therefore, we have chosen party preferences as our third independent variable. However, we are primarily interested in the so-called party winners/losers, rather than preferences for individual parties, testing a hypothesis that voters whose parties have formed the government (party winners) tend to be more satisfied than opposition voters, i.e. party losers (Anderson & Guillory 1997, Anderson & Tverdova 2001, Linde & Ekman 2003).

5.2 Normative models of a democratic public space

Representative government is the cornerstone of practically all modern democratic regimes. This relatively recent "invention" made it possible to overcome traditional democracy's fundamental obstacle as we know it from Greek city-states or Rousseau and other classics' ideas, i.e. the necessity to limit the number of participants in decision making and the area governed in order to make it manageable. Such change brings forward the relationship between representatives and the represented, one that crucially determines the functioning of the democratic process. Representative democracy means, on one hand, stronger public influence on politics and, on the other hand, the public's displacement (alienation). Displacement arises out of the division of political labor and is a necessary condition for democratic mass politics to function. Professional bureaucratic politics, as one aspect of the "iron cage" of modernity (Weber), is characteristic for modern society. It is based on the formal rationality of expert knowledge and, just like other narrowly specialized activities, perceived by ordinary people as distant, boring, and accessible to a small circle of people — experts and politicians, and perhaps journalists, officials, and social scientists as well. In a representative democracy, the direct involvement of citizens in most political decision making processes is practically impossible (and indeed undesirable). This is due to various technical and factual reasons: as opposed to classic democracies, most policy problems are not simple enough for a citizen assembly to solve. The development of communication technologies (e-democracy) cannot replace expert knowledge and skills. Decision making is restricted to a limited number of elected professional politicians who are supervised through periodic elections in which political elites compete. The general public is a group actor which, by making its choice, gives elites consent to govern and supervises their actions to make sure elites follow the group's — or public — interest.

5.2.1 The representative liberal model of public space

This broad concept embraces a range of normative models of democracy that take the existence of public space as desirable but believe that people's participation in governance should be indirect and limited. On one side of the continuum, there are models based on John Locke's liberalism such as J. Bentham and J. Mill's protective democracy or J. S. Mill and A. de Tocqueville's developmental democracy. The other side of the continuum is represented by models that "appease" classic elitism with democracy (Hloušek & Kopeček 2003), and above all, Schumpeter's concept of democracy along with the more recent concepts of A. Downs or W. Kornhauser (Ferree et al. 2002). It also includes G. Sartori's "realist" concept of democracy which emphasizes quality leadership.

In the representative model, citizens' interests are articulated through representative institutions (elections and political parties). While direct democracy is not deemed feasible in modern society, the opportunity of **free electoral choice** between different parties (or between competing elites in the school of democratic elitism) on a regular basis is considered sufficient guarantee of democracy. Political participation is basically limited to the act of choosing representatives because any greater involvement by people in governance processes would undermine the political system's stability and equilibrium that is ensured by educated, informed, motivated, and responsible elites. Active participation by people who are generally uninformed and apathetic would lead to rushed, short-sighted, and simply bad decisions and policies. From this perspective, the public is a mass whose actions and attitudes may contradict the very democratic values and principles (such as the protection of minorities from the tyranny of the majority) and must be regulated by the educated and capable elites. The public space is governed by elites—mass leaders whose portion of power reflects diverse interests within society in line with the **proportionality principle**. According to this principle, the more people a given party or organization represents, the higher its portion of power and media coverage should be.

Such a symbiotic relationship between elites and general public would be impossible without a relatively high **elite autonomy**, a key principle of liberal democracy as well as modern elite theories. Proponents of the so-called demo-elitism emphasize that elite autonomy is important in relation to the general public as well as among elites themselves. Too close links between the different elite groups undermine their independence and ability to supervise each other (Etzioni-Halevy 1990, 1993). At the same time, the required high autonomy of policy makers (or, more broadly, elites) depends on transparent and responsible exercise of power in terms of clearly presenting one's attitudes and assuming responsibility for decisions taken. In other words, the public lends to its elected representatives not only the power to decide, but also sufficient discretion and time to put through and implement their decisions. However, accountability is another inherent aspect of elite autonomy. Elites are accountable to the public, which decides whether or not they will be kept in power.

Even educated and informed elites cannot govern without the aid of experts in a given subject matter (health care system, defense, education, etc.) or in the political process itself.[58] Rather than informing the general public, the role of these experts is to provide expertise to elected representatives who are capable of understanding the subject matter and are competent to make decisions. Elected representatives are chosen and paid in order to decide in ways beneficial to the general public. Once they reach a decision, public debate is considered closed and moves on to other issues that are still open. Long, aimless debates without clear decisions taken jeopardize elites themselves because they may call into question their ability to decide efficiently and beneficially (Ferree et al. 2002).

The representative model of democracy gives individuals — and the public as a whole — unprecedented opportunities to influence their country's politics and participate in governance. At the same time, it is criticized both from the perspective of classic democratic theory (representative democracy is not genuine democracy) and by proponents of modern participative democracy models who believe it undermines fundamental democratic principles (political power in the hands of a small elite group) and deprives individuals of freedom and responsibility for their own actions and, ultimately, of their values and opinions. The public is nothing but a mass that, from time to time, may

---

58 Communication advisers are another group of experts who aid politicians to get elected (election campaign, media presentation, etc.) and remain in hold of the acquired positions (crisis management).

turn into a crowd. The limited opportunities to participate in the exercise of power prevent the growth of a "genuine" democratic public, one that is capable of pursuing its interests responsibly.

5.2.2 The participative model of public space

Proponents of the participative model advance the idea that the general public should have more direct influence on decision making processes than is offered by representative democracy. An individual should have the right to take part in the activities of their political community and efficient decision making about the collective future through collective action. Communitarism, associative democracy, and direct democracy, as the main schools of thought, are primarily differentiated by their different emphases on minimizing the importance of representative institutions. A special case is represented by the recently influential discursive/deliberative model by J. Habermas (1984), J. Bessette (1980, 1994) and other scholars such as J. Cohen, A. Gutmann, and J. Fishskin.

The main principle of participative democracy can be characterized as broadening and strengthening **public autonomy** by political means such as referenda, citizen-based policy making, public debates, and participation in strategy formulation. This ultimately results in greater control of the general public over elites. Furthermore, demands for empowering lower-level public administration and increasing people's opportunities to participate directly can be found in different forms and combinations. Participative democracy scholars believe that this model facilitates the fact that responsibility for decisions is extended to all citizens as their commitment to society. **Political competence** develops in the general public, which results in better common decisions. Political preferences and abilities to consider public affairs arise out of debates within the public space and, more generally, as a product of the political process, rather than *a priori,* based on group membership (age, education, income, etc.). By facilitating full and **active citizenship,** participation transforms individuals into citizens and mass into public (Barber 1984).

By stimulating empathy between groups with different interests, participative democracy improves the shared political culture. Conflict resolution between social groups occurs openly and as a non-zero-sum game (Pierre & Peters 2000). The political system should further respect individual autonomy because "an ordinary person can better judge what is good for them than any self-appointed elite". This changes the role of experts considerably, making them primarily responsible for uncovering social inequalities that are (re)produced by different social, political, and cultural traditions, and empowering disadvantaged groups in order to recognize and assert their interests. The effort to provide objective expertise as we know it from the representative model is complemented by an **advocacy dimension** or rejected altogether. Proponents of participative democracy are also rather suspicious ofclosing public debate by the time a decision is taken. From their point of view, such closure might often be premature, resulting in a pseudo-consensus, especially when it comes to non-routine decisions that require answering important normative questions. In such cases, continuing public debate should gradually result in a consensus or at least working compromise (Ferree et al. 2002). The Table 5.2 summarizes the principal characteristics of both models.

Table 5.2: Characteristics of the representative and participative models

	Representative	Participative
Public participation	Periodic but limited, passive	Continuous, encouraged, active
Decision competence	Belongs to elites	Arises out of close public-elite cooperation. General public decides directly in some cases.
Value of democracy	Instrumental and procedural	Intrinsic – ends as well as means
Views on bureaucracy	Optimistic – trusted and competent	Skeptical – non-representative, pursuing own interest
Principal interest	Effectiveness and stability, rational choice	Accountability vis-à-vis public interest, individual growth
Principal forms of participation	Election and approval of representatives	Diverse; local level is the most efficient and rational
Views on general public	Skeptical – apathetic, easily manipulated	Optimistic – informed, clever, and active
Public space	Free marketplace of ideas; objective expertise; effort to close debate; majority principle	Empowering disadvantaged groups; public debates; dialogue and mutual respect; effort to reach consensus; respect for minorities

Sources: Steelman (2001) and Ferree et al. (2002), adapted by author.

The above information might suggest that the representative and participative models and their proponents are in sharp conflict with each other. However, such an interpretation would be simplifying and one might even say that both models "fight the same enemy", i.e. populist democracy. Democratic elitism tells us that the tyranny of masses can be averted through liberal democracy, when educated, responsible, and accountable representatives are in power. According to Kornhauser, pluralist society is different from mass society in that the former supports liberal democracy, controlling access to power through institutional procedures and mediating elements, while the latter tends to allow more direct and unlimited access to power (Kornhauser 1960). As noted by Riker (1982), the power of liberal democracy lies in the fact that it does not require permanent popular involvement in governance in order to legitimize ruling political authorities.

Participative model scholars fear populism as well, but see its roots in elites themselves. Rather than protectors of democracy, elites are seen as manipulators striving to impose their power over the masses and abuse power positions for their own personal interests. Powerless masses can be transformed into a pluralist and self-confident public by getting involved in decision making (learning democracy through participation rather than merely education). Even the most enlightened elites cannot rule by themselves. The instruments of participative and direct democracy should thus be understood as complements, rather than substitutes to representative democracy. They remain mere instruments that may or may not be applied in a democratic way. E.g. Hayward (1996) differentiates between a plebiscite and a referendum, demonstrating that the plebiscite is a pseudo-democratic, populist instrument that is applied to manipulate the masses rather than let the public think and decide.[59] The roots of such distinction are deeper and go back to Weber's concept of plebiscitary democracy as an important link between charismatic and bureaucratic leadership (see Frič et al., 2008, for more details).

5.2.3 Which model is preferred by the Czech elites and general public?

Preferences for given models of democracy were studied by means of asking a battery of conflicting statements representing their principal dimensions (see Table 5.3) and aggregating the results into one single

---

59 Hayward (1996) differentiates between referenda and plebiscites based on two criteria: which level (top or bottom) initiated the process and whether the question addressed refers to a specific issue or rather constitutes a blank check for actions envisaged by existing government. While these two aspects might be difficult to determine, as a rule, referenda are initiated from the bottom and address specific issues related to a principal constitutional, territorial, or national decision. Populist plebiscites cover the opposite cases (ibid, 16).

index. This method is advantageous in that individual statements indicate various processes and institutions in more detail, representing the two models' principal conflicts. Respondents consider specific dimensions, rather than mere labels (representative versus participative democracy), which would have little intersubjective reliability.

Table 5.3: Operationalizing principal dimensions of both models of democracy in CESES surveys

	Representative	**Participative**
Public participation	It is sufficient that people take part in regular elections and elect their representatives.	Mere election participation is not sufficient. People should continuously strive to influence their elected representatives' decision making.
Decision competence	Elected representatives should decide on their own, without bothering the general public with their problems.	People affected by a decision should take an active part in its making.
Principal interest	Decisions should primarily be economically beneficial.	Decisions should primarily be socially just.
Principal forms of participation	Only political parties should assert people's interests.	In order to assert their interests, people should associate beyond political parties as well.
Public space	A minority must conform to the majority.	Minority interests should be also taken into account in decision making.

Source: Author.

A large majority of both elites and the general public agree on dimensions representing people's active involvement in the political process, i.e. activity between elections, asserting interests also outside political parties, and taking an active part in decision making on public affairs. In contrast, elites and the general public hold conflicting views on the social justice versus economic rationales for decision making and whether minority views should be taken into consideration. Elites and the general public are split into two commensurate groups on these two dimensions. The economic rationale and majority decision making tend to be supported by the economic and media elites along with ODS voters. In contrast, the social justice rationale and respect for minority views are more often preferred by the civic and cultural elites along with the aggregate group of voters of other parliamentary parties. In terms of political orientation, the economic rationale is clearly supported by

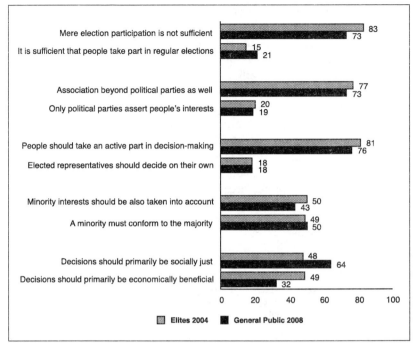

Figure 5.1: Distribution of each dimension of the representative-participative model (per cent)
Sources: CESES 2007, 2008.
Note: Don't knows and non-responses add up to 100%.

self-declared right-wing respondents (such a relationship is much weaker even if statistically significant for minorities[60]).

The general public is similarly split on the above two dimensions but in the latter case, social justice strongly predominates over economic benefits. Interestingly, these preferences are little influenced by socio-economic status or voter preferences. Substantial differences are only found for the economic rationale, which is most preferred by ODS voters and non-voters, while social justice is most preferred by KSČM voters. With this latter exception, these are universal principles of decision making in society upon which the general public tends to agree without deviations.

---

60 In the former case of economic benefits versus social justice, correlation coefficient equals to −0.35. In the latter case of respecting minority views versus conforming to the majority, CC is as little as −0.18. Negative values are based on our coding of political orientation (from 1 = left to 10 = right).

What is the optimum decision making procedure and related responsibility for decisions taken? We presented elite respondents with three principal forms of democratic decision making and asked them to choose one that best fit their preferences. For the sake of our survey, each model was expressed as briefly as possible, through its main attributes (e.g. elected representatives and their accountability; consulting important decisions; referenda). In the subsequent general public survey, we left out two of the three models and, for the sake of intelligibility, only studied the level of people's agreement with direct democracy. While this approach precluded direct comparison because of different wordings, we believe our results outline some fundamental differences between elites and the general public in their preferences for each model of democracy.

Table 5.4: Distribution of preferences for different models of democracy by elite segments and the general public

Elite segment/ Decision making procedure	Elites 2007			General Public 2008[61]
	Representative democracy (parliamentary[a])	Participative democracy (mixed)[b]	Direct democracy[c]	Direct democracy[c]
Political	44%	35%	20%	75%
Administrative	46%	42%	9%	
Economic	46%	42%	9%	
Media	39%	50%	11%	
Security	39%	53%	8%	
Cultural	27%	61%	9%	
Civic	22%	64%	12%	
Total	**37%**	**50%**	**11%**	

Sources: CESES 2007, 2008.

Note: Row percentages (Don't knows and non-responses add up to 100%). Modal categories are highlighted in grey.

[a] "I favor a democracy in which the general public elects its representatives into parliament and the parliament takes responsibility for political decisions."

[b] "I favor a democracy in which important government and parliament decisions are consulted with the general public and representatives of civil society organizations."

[c] "I favor a democracy in which political decisions are taken by referendum as much as possible."

---

61 The former question that was used in our elite survey and distinguished between three forms of democratic decision making was simplified for the purpose of our general public survey into preference for one single form, i.e. referendum (direct democracy).

The participative model of democracy is supported by most elites, and in particular, members of the civic and cultural segments. The representative model is most preferred by the political, economic, and administrative elites. Members of the public administration are most trusted by the political and administrative elites (as well as the security elites). This means that the policy making elites are somewhat reluctant to allow the general public more participation in decision making as a result of their positive views of bureaucracy, rather than a skeptical view of the general public (the latter is less shared among elites). We can also assume that elites view the possible introduction of participative elements in decision making processes as a complication of the decision making process that curtails their autonomy and jeopardizes their privileges.

Although participative democracy is a winner among elites, it is clear that they prefer a model which relies on representative democracy. Elements of participation can be built into the model but participation by the general public (and other actors) is limited to information and consultation. Referendum, as a principal aspect of direct democracy, is supported by a minority of elites. Introduction and "maximum possible use" of referenda would substantially alter the political institutional regime in terms of lower control over the decision making process. Thus, it is little surprising that current elites are reluctant to support such a change. However, their preference of a given model of democracy and rejection of referenda cannot be explained merely as unwillingness to change the *status quo* and harm their own interests. Undoubtedly, elite members' attitudes and beliefs on what is desirable or right, and about the general public as a political actor, are factors as well. Elites' cautious view of the referendum may be caused by their fear of referendum abuse by populists of all kinds as well as by elites' lack of confidence in themselves and their own leadership skills. Czech elites do not believe that the general public might act as a responsible political actor who is capable of taking decisions based on factual knowledge (see below). At the same time, they realize a referendum would reveal the fact that Czech elites themselves are often unsuccessful leaders by failing to persuade the general public that certain decisions are right and beneficial (see more in Frič et al. 2008).

Our data do not unambiguously support or reject the hypothesized value/ideological versus interest-based preference for decision making procedures, and both of these motives clearly apply at given times and situations. Distribution by party preferences demonstrates that highest support for the traditional representative democracy is given by voters of the ODS, the strongest coalition party in 2007 and a party that was ideologically closer to that model than other parties. ODS voters as party winners did not support any large institutional change. In contrast, voters of the KSČM, which was relatively strong in the Chamber of Deputies but had almost no coalition potential at a national level, and thus was pushed to the political periphery, expressed a relatively high support for changing the *status quo*, even in favor of direct democracy. Coalition government membership might also explain the relatively low referendum support among voters of the Greens, despite the party's broad explicit support for direct democracy.

Table 5.5: Distribution of elite preferences for different models of democracy by party preferences

Party chosen in last lower chamber election/ Decision making procedure	Representative democracy (parliamentary)[a]	Participative democracy (mixed)[b]	Direct democracy[c]	N
ODS	53%	40%	5%	383
ČSSD	24%	61%	15%	162
KDU-ČSL	26%	61%	11%	88
KSČM	11%	46%	43%	37
Greens	27%	57%	12%	84

Source: CESES 2007.
Note: Row percentages (Don't knows and non-responses add up to 100%). Modal categories are highlighted in grey (two most frequent categories with only 3 percentage point difference are highlighted for KSČM voters).
[a] "I favor a democracy in which the general public elects its representatives into parliament and the parliament takes responsibility for political decisions."
[b] "I favor a democracy in which important government and parliament decisions are consulted with the general public and representatives of civil society organizations."
[c] "I favor a democracy in which political decisions are taken by referendum as much as possible."

As opposed to elites, the general public strongly supports direct democracy. The Czech Republic thus follows a trend we know from Western European countries where voices for greater public participation or even direct democracy have been on the rise. A question remains whether these calls for greater public participation are related to support for democracy and its principles. Dalton, Bürklin & Drummond (2001) persuasively argue that higher support of direct democracy is linked to growing public discontent with politics, rather than Western societies' leaning to postmaterialist values. The authors reject the hypothesis that greater and more direct participation will be preferred by more educated and politically "sophisticated" citizens (as a result of the so-called social modernization). Instead, they use Eurobarometer data to demonstrate that direct democracy is most supported by people with lower education and those who declared themselves little informed. Similar evidence on the support for direct democracy can be found in the Czech Republic (e.g. Frič et al. 2003). Differences between socio-economic groups make it apparent that direct democracy is least supported by people with highest status,[62] who can be assumed to have the most educated, knowledgeable about politics, and interested in public affairs.

5.3 Democracy and democratic support

New political and economic systems were established after the collapse of communist regimes in countries of Central and Eastern Europe. Their parliaments adopted new or amended constitutions, governments gradually retreated from economies, which were transformed from planned to market-based systems. However, a mere formal implementation of new order does not guarantee its functionality. The working of new institutions must be verified in everyday political and economic "routine". People's belief that the new regime solves the society's problems better is an important element of stability and sustainability of democratic political systems. Regime stability and sustainability can only be achieved if elites are willing to play the (political) game by the rules and the new institutional regime is supported by the general public (Jacobs 2001, Pollack et al. 2001). In other words, the political regime must enjoy people's support in order to survive.

While not exclusive, political support is perceived as one of the principal determinants of democratic stability (e.g. Easton 1975, 1979; Rose, Mishler & Haerpfer 1998, Norris 1999).[63] Public support legitimizes new political institutions and makes them more resistant to

---

62 21% rather or strongly disagree; chi-square=18.4, differences are statistically significant at a 0.03 confidence level.

63 Social inequalities, elite attitudes and actions, the existence and performance of democratic institutions, and other factors play a role as well. Therefore, the specific circumstances of simultaneously changing political, economic, and social regimes during transformation and consolidation require that we also analyze economic attitudes, social attitudes, and value orientations.

threats external (e.g. war) and internal alike (e.g. economic crisis, social inequalities, coup d'état). It lowers the risk of unconventional actions aimed at removing the existing elites and, in particular, political violence. It is furthermore important for the system's performance because high trust empowers governments to make decisions without the additional cost of enforcement or garnering special support for every important decision (Mishler and Rose 1999). Government performance may thus lead to higher support, which results in a "democratic spiral" of growing performance and support (Gamson 1968). Conversely, diminishing support lowers performance which, in turn, causes further decline of support in a downward spiral.

The hypothesis of political culture scholars that public attitudes importantly affect the political system's stability[64] is built upon by David Easton in his concept of political support (Easton 1975, 1979), which distinguishes between three objects of public support (the political community, the political regime, and ruling political authorities) and two types of support (specific and diffuse). Easton argues that internalized membership in a given political community and agreement with the values, norms, and institutions of a given political regime (diffuse support) are, in the long-term, more important for democracy than the short-term (specific) support of ruling authorities and their politics. It is only the diffuse type of support that, according to Easton, indicates a political system's long-term stability.

The above conceptual model can be favorably applied in studying support for democracy in countries with long traditions of democratic culture where democratic values and principles are subject to socialization from early childhood and people basically have no other direct experience than the one with their democratic regime. However, in new democracies, evaluations of existing political systems and their representatives may be based on different factors. Some political support depends on social-cultural or economic factors but also on the role of elites in the processes of transformation and democratic consolidation. As opposed to traditional democracies, transforming regimes are subject to much stronger political and social pressures, lack established institutions and experienced elites. The idea of differential (hierarchical) political support based on political stability thus becomes relevant under these specific circumstances of political system transformations.

---

64 According to Almond & Verba (1963), individual political attitudes (evaluations, knowledge, and views of political events) influence one's political behavior and carry out different functions in the political system. In their entirety, these attitudes form the country's political culture.

Transformational political elites depend on short-term but strong public support legitimizing their efforts. While such short-term support can be earned through positive economic performance, in the long term it has to change into a diffuse support of the political system as such (independent of momentary economic and social situation). In Central and Eastern European countries, former socialist regimes were legitimized through social security and government-sponsored services. Economic downturn thus may critically jeopardize the legitimacy of a market economy and the democratic political regime, especially on the part of the general public that is losing economically under the new regime. From this perspective, not only attitudes to the new regime, but also to the old (authoritative) one are key. Strong representation of people supporting the old regime in society may jeopardize democracy and it is only these people's "re-socialization" towards supporting democracy and rejecting authoritarianism that can ensure safe diffuse support that is independent of economic and political crises. Such re-socialization may occur during the authoritarian regime's transformation into democracy, through the "consolidation effect" (Torcal, Brusattin, Martín and Kakepaki 2005).

Some doubts are raised by the strict distinction between attitudes/ orientations to political authorities and those to the political regime and its institutions. As noted by Steen (2001), some institutions may be identified by their representatives. This begs the question, to what extent does political support depend on the "institutional aura" that the elite members receive from institutions they run, on one hand, and the charisma the institutions receive from their top representatives, on the other hand. Therefore, the line between institutions and authorities representing them is likely to be somewhat fuzzy in all modern societies. In post-communist countries with relatively young or emerging democratic institutions, we may assume a much stronger identification of institutions with their representatives, and thus, stronger interactions between the specific and diffuse forms of political support. A decline in specific support thus may result in a much sharper fall of diffuse support, relatively to countries with long democratic traditions. In other words, dissatisfaction with ruling elites may jeopardize support for democracy as a suitable political regime for times of economic/social prosperity and crisis alike.

But has political support the same importance in the case of elites themselves? Even for elites, acceptance and support of democratic principles and institutions is a strong determinant of the ways conflicts between competing interests in society are solved and of democratic stability in general. However, elites have to do more than just accept the rules of the game and support existing institutions. Given their specific leadership role, democratic theory foresees that elites should be, to some extent, interested in public support. Elites cannot act as fully autonomous actors and, therefore, are obliged to seek and garner public support to legitimize their power positions in society. Given the nature of representative democracy, interaction with the general public is most essential for elites that are active within the political system. However, it is necessary for other elite segments as well since they are to some extent dependent on public support, be it indirectly (through politics) or directly. The question of power position legitimacy is relevant in cases like private property, the role of science or religion in society, trust in the independence and effectiveness of public administration, etc. The nature of mutual relations within the elite (between elite segments) is another factor of democratic system stability (e.g. Higley & Burton 1997; Higley & Lengyel 2000; Etzioni-Halevy 1993, Ruostetsaari 2006). Chapter 2 investigates the issue of elite structural integration in more detail.

As we suggested above, political support is the underlying concept for our empirical measurement of general public and elites' political orientations and attitudes. **Political support** measures positive evaluations of political objects at the individual level. Among modern concepts of political support, we focus on David Easton's distinction between three objects of political support (political community, political regime, and political authorities) and two types of support (specific and diffuse). This general concept has been used in most contemporary empirical studies of political support (e.g. Fuchs 1993; Klingemann 1998; Dalton 2004). Easton's as well as other two-dimensional taxonomies of political support usually distinguish between object-related attitudes and modes of support. Norris (1999) offers a different approach in that she connects objects and modes of support into one dimension in which the specific and diffuse support form a single continuum in order to assess each object's level of specific/diffuse support.

Both approaches have their advocates and critics, raising numerous questions. Do ordinary citizens distinguish between the different objects of political support (authorities, regime, community) or do their attitudes arise out of specific sources in order to become generalized across objects? For instance, can we separate support for a country's incumbent president from support for the presidential office as such? 1970s and 1980s studies carried out in the U.S. (Miller 1974) and Germany (Muller & Jukam 1977; Muller, Jukam & Seligson 1982; and others) demonstrate that the different levels of political support are strongly correlated.

In this chapter, we side with Torcal, Montero, and Gunther's view of political support as a multi-dimensional phenomenon that is shaped by multiple factors (Torcal & Montero 2006; Montero, Gunther & Torcal 1998). The most frequently used indicators of political support form three conceptually and empirically separate attitude clusters: democratic support, political discontent, and political disaffection. However, rather than seeking relationships between the different clusters of political support, the goal of this chapter will be to analyze differences within the elites as well as between the different elite categories and status groups in the general public.

5.3.1 Democratic support

Actors' attitudes to the political regime constitute a fundamental element of political culture and indicate relationship to existing social order. A lack of consensus about the "rules of the game" perpetuates instability of the state. In order to understand the nature of general public's attitudes to the political regime and ongoing decision making processes, it is essential to distinguish between general support for the political regime and discontent with the regime's current performance. Every government is sometimes incapable of fulfilling the public's expectations, be in the short or long term. Every democracy thus experiences periodic swings of satisfaction and dissatisfaction with the government and political elites in general. While political decisions, public policies and programs, and, ultimately governments come and go, the political regime should rest on a reservoir of stable generalized (diffuse) support, one that does not depend on current achievements or failures of the government and its policies.

Support for the political regime or democracy is usually measured in public opinion surveys by the question whether democracy is the best form of government. This is the way democratic support is measured by surveys like the *World Values Survey* or *Eurobarometer*. However, as Mishler and Rose (1999, 2001) inform us, this question has little validity for new, transitory, or incomplete democratic regimes because their people's ideas about democracy and its principles are rather vague. Therefore, these authors recommend a more realistic and more valid measurement of democratic support through a question comparing current regime with the former (undemocratic) one. By assessing the regimes respondents have experienced, the authors wish to avoid ambiguous understandings and abstract concepts.

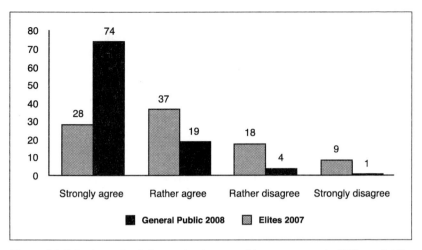

Figure 5.2: Was the societal change that happened in our country in 1989 worth it?
Sources: CESES 2007, 2008.
Note: Don't knows and non-responses add up to 100%.

An overwhelming majority of elites approve of the societal change and, by doing so, clearly prefer democracy from the preceding authoritarian regime. KSČM voters are the only elite group rejecting the new regime (58% rather disagree and 14% strongly disagree) and a relatively high representation of these voters is responsible for the slightly under-average support for current regime among members of the political elite. All other elites show high levels of support for the current regime, only differing in the strength of their support. Above all, party losers (ČSSD voters and non-voters) and people more than 45 years old show somewhat weaker support.

As opposed to elites, members the general public are much more differentiated in their evaluations of the societal change and, thus, support for democracy as a preferable political regime. People with the highest socio-economic status and ODS voters tend to express strong agreement (43% and 63% strongly agree, respectively). Furthermore, regime change is generally supported by people with higher ISEI and coalition party voters. In contrast, people with the lowest ISEI and KSČM voters oppose the current regime (15% and 34% strongly disagree, respectively).

Do elites really find democracy "the only game in town" (Linz & Stepan 1996: 5), i.e. are their political orientations coherent with

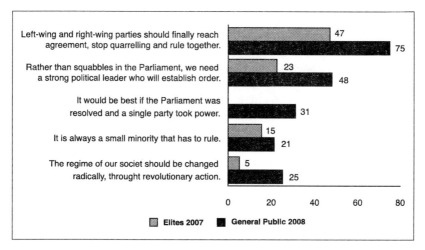

Left-wing and right-wing parties should finally reach agreement, stop quarrelling and rule together. 47 / 75

Rather than squabbles in the Parliament, we need a strong political leader who will establish order. 23 / 48

It would be best if the Parliament was resolved and a single party took power. 31

It is always a small minority that has to rule. 15 / 21

The regime of our societ should be changed radically, throught revolutionary action. 5 / 25

0   20   40   60   80

Elites 2007   General Public 2008

Figure 5.3: Selected attitudes coherent with democracy
Sources: CESES 2007, 2008.
Note: Values represent the percentages of respondents who strongly agree or rather agree.

democratic principles and do they find democratic institutions an efficient means of solving conflicts within society? Or vice versa, do they reject undemocratic procedures and principles as unacceptable "shortcuts" to solving social problems? And what are the views of the general public?

The statement that "the regime of our society should be changed radically, through revolutionary action" met with the strongest disagreement among elites. The necessity of a radical change in our society is strongly rejected by elites of all segments, voter preferences, and ages. Small differences exist in the strength of disagreement, with KSČM voters and, surprisingly, also the economic elites expressing weaker disagreement (6% rather agree and "only" 66% strongly disagree). While a certain leaning to radical change is understandable for KSČM voters, we can only speculate about its reasons in the case of economic elites.

In contrast, a part of the general public certainly has nothing against revolutionary change. As much as one-third of respondents agree with the idea of resolving the Parliament and a single party taking power,[65] mostly people with lower ISEI and KSČM voters. The relationship with status groups is significant but not particularly strong. These attitudes

---

65   The question was not asked in the 2007 elite survey.

are also relatively frequent for people with the highest socio-economic status (27% agree with Parliament resolution and single party rule, 19% agree with revolutionary change). This comparison and the elite-public comparison make it clear that, on one hand, agreement with undemocratic ways of changing society is partially determined by socio-economic status but, on the other hand, elite membership also plays an important role. The question remains whether this is caused by elite members' stronger democratic character or their resistance to a more radical change that would likely make them lose their current positions.

The Czech elites and general public also refuse the elitist idea that only a small group of people should rule. They probably associate minority rule with the concept of an oligarchy, as opposed to representative democracy. Both regimes involve the rule of a minority. However, in a representative democracy, this minority is elected, and therefore it is accountable to the public and can be forced to resign. In contrast, oligarchy does not abide by democratic principles and the minority uses different means of legitimizing its positions (such as their wealth or divine mandate). While elites and the general public agree in this respect, our data reveals an interesting paradox. While KSČM voters among elites most strongly oppose the rule of minority (81% strongly disagreed), it is this party's voters among the general public who, along with lower ISEI respondents, most frequently support the statement (36% strongly or rather agree). We interpret this discrepancy by the fact that elites (and in particular, political elites, of which 65% are KSČM voters) are much more politically sophisticated and, at least from an ideological perspective, find oligarchy unacceptable. At the same time, amongst the general public, the rule of a minority is most frequently supported by people who are discontented with the current situation, feel politically and socially marginalized, are skeptical about democracy and do not believe that political representatives are fulfilling people's mandate.

Relatively to the rule of a minority, members of the general public and some elites are much more responsive to the calls for a strong political leader who would assert his authority and establish order. Such a "shortcut" in the often difficult and lengthy ways of solving problems by parliamentary means is supported by almost half of the general public and more than one-fifth of elites. Once again, it is the KSČM (as well as ČSSD) voters and people with the lowest ISEI who most frequently call for a strong leader. Among elites, this tends to be supported by security elites, KSČM supporters, and in particular, those who did not vote in the last elections. Preference for a strong leader is a manifestation of authoritarian tendencies that emphasize security over freedom — which necessarily produces more uncertainty, lengthy negotiations, and frequent compromises that may, for instance, complicate the work of security forces or prevent the solution of marginalized people's problems. Non-voters tend to be discontented with the functioning of democracy and democratic institutions in the Czech Republic. (see below) In contrast, a strong leader is strictly rejected by coalition party voters (among elites and the general public alike), ones who clearly prefer democratic ways of conflict resolution, even at the expense of lower efficiency and security. A strong leader is also not supported by the administrative and cultural elites. While respondents with the highest ISEI hold the least different attitudes, compared to elites, the difference is still substantial.

While most Czech elite members do not like the idea of a strong leader, almost half of them do not advocate another solution, one that is even found in some of Western Europe's established democracies: shared rule by left-wing and right-wing parties in the form of a grand coalition or "oppositional treaty" (the Czech Republic has already tried out the latter solution). In proportional electoral systems, shared left-right rule can make it more efficient to adopt laws and policies requiring a strong consensus (such as pension system reform). On the other hand, it puts in question the very essence of political competition (a conflict of ideas) which, especially at the time of economic downturn, may cause the rise of populist leaders searching for outside enemies, etc. It also raises the risk of state-owned and state-sponsored companies being colonized and their financial profits being transferred to lobbyists and political parties themselves in an extent even greater than nowadays. The relationship between a grand coalition government and public administration is also problematic because big coalitions tend to divide public offices among the coalition parties and maintain such a *status quo* for as long as possible. This trend is further solidified by the lack of law on civil service in the Czech Republic — a law whose date of taking effect has been repeatedly deferred. It is probably this concern that makes the administrative elites the strongest opponents of shared left-right rule. Party winners, and in particular ODS voters, are similarly strongly opposed. In contrast, most party losers along with more than 50% of non-voters do not oppose a grand coalition. Shared left-right rule enjoys the strongest support in the general public, and in particular, among left-wing voters and people with lower ISEI (more than four-fifths). While people with the highest ISEI (and coalition party voters) show the least support to this form of government, their support is still much stronger compared to elites.

5.3.2 Satisfaction with politics and political authorities

Numerous surveys demonstrate that democracy as a lived reality always enjoys weaker support than democracy as an ideal. This applies to new democracies and, perhaps even more, to established Western democracies. The key questions at this level of support are: how is the given political regime functioning in practice? What is the regime's performance? The efficiency of a political regime in supplying public goods is an important factor in its legitimacy, whether or not the regime is democratic (Linde & Ekman 2003). Regime performance can be assessed in many areas such as protection of free speech, individual rights, or minority rights. However, economic performance and evaluations of the ruling authorities (the government) are used most often.

Satisfaction with the functioning of democracy measures evaluations of current democratic governance processes and respondents' attitudes to their country's "constitutional reality" (Fuchs, Guidorossi & Svenson 1995). It is thus a mixed indicator of diffuse and specific support. While the indicator is evaluative by nature, the respondent evaluates the performance of an entire political regime, rather than its momentary outcomes. Thomassen (1995: 383) has precisely this in mind when he says

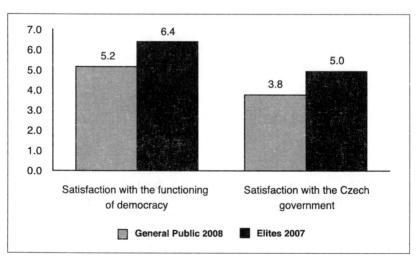

Figure 5.4: Satisfaction with the functioning of democracy and the Czech government
Sources: CESES 2007, 2008.
Note: Values represent average ratings on a scale from 1 (absolutely dissatisfied) to 10 (absolutely satisfied).

that satisfaction with democracy measures "a felt discrepancy between democratic norms and the actual democratic process". It is thus little surprising that the lowest level of satisfaction is expressed by civic elites, who presumably share higher standards of democratic functioning, and therefore, are more critical in assessing the state of democracy vis-à-vis the ideal. However, little satisfied are also the KSČM voters and non-voters, who may feel their interests to be insufficiently represented under current regime, whether because of other political parties' reluctance to cooperate with the Communists or a general lack of alternatives to current political parties. In contrast, ODS voters and administrative elites are strongly satisfied, probably because democracy seems to be working according to their expectations.

As expected, the general public tends to be less satisfied with democracy, even though the under-one-point difference between elites' and the general public's evaluations is a rather small difference given the 10-point scale. Similarly to elites, KSČM voters (averaging 3.7 points), ČSSD voters (4.8 points), and non-voters (4.7 points) are the least satisfied groups of the general public. This result conforms the hypothesis that party winners tend to be more satisfied than party losers, whether in Western democratic regimes (Anderson & Guillory 1997) or in the new post-socialist ones (Anderson & Tverdova 2001, Linde & Ekman 2003). People with the lowest ISEI also tend to be dissatisfied with democracy (average rating 4.6) but even people with the highest socio-economic status do not reach the same levels of satisfaction as elites.

The second question, satisfaction with the government, measures evaluations of the political regime's performance and current outcomes, i.e. everyday activities by politicians and government institutions. As opposed to democracy as an ideal and lived reality, the government is the most specific object of political support and, at the same time, the one drawing the most criticism by citizens and elites alike. This also applies to the Czech Republic. A comparison further reveals that the difference in satisfaction between elites and the general public is greater than in the case of satisfaction with democracy. The best ratings for the elite's government are given by the administrative and security elites, which belong to the establishment and are, therefore, practically rating their own performance. A comparison by party preferences reveals that the more critical government ratings by the political elites partially depend on their government representation, with coalition party voters giving different ratings than opposition voters. Furthermore, voters of the two smaller coalition parties are more critical than ODS voters.

A similar distribution of (the predominantly negative) government ratings exists in the general public. ODS voters (4.9), followed by voters of the two other coalition parties, constitute the only groups of relatively satisfied citizens. KSČM voters (2.7) and people with the lowest ISEI (3.3) are the least satisfied. See Chapter 3 for a more detailed analysis of people's evaluations of different areas of life (economic competition, protections of rights and human dignity, corruption, and political competition).

5.3.3 Political disaffection

Many different kinds of elite-public relations have emerged in democratic societies over time. Such relations may be formal — regulated by laws — or informal, based on the given society's tradition and (political) culture. Whatever form the relations take, they are affected by the basic premise of democracy, i.e. that public preferences are reflected in political outcomes (Manza & Cook 2002). This taken-for-granted premise is, however, complicated by modern democracies' representative regimes, with the decisive role of representatives and their understandings of what accountability to voters and the society means. Democratic theory offers two basic perspectives on the ways elected representatives should respond to public opinion. In the **mandate/delegate view**, voters give their mandate to delegates, who should aim at reflecting voters' preferences (McCrone & Kuklinski 1979). Representatives are mere means and servants that are subordinated to those who elected them into office. In any case, they are expected to follow their voters' interest exclusively, rather than their own interest (Pitkin 1967). From this perspective, public opinion as expressed through different channels (elections, research surveys, interest group actions) should play a decisive role in formulating public policies and deciding important issues. Policy makers should carefully consider and obey the "dictate" of public opinion (Foyle 1999).

In contrast, the **trustee view** foresees a much greater autonomy for elected representatives. These should primarily rely on their own judgment, rather than the most likely uninformed opinion of their voters and the general public as a whole. Regular elections are practically the only opportunity for public opinion to be expressed in order to elect the best, who will then act in public interest (Foyle 1999). Listening to the *vox populi* at other times is unwise, undesirable, and illegitimate.

An attentive reader certainly noticed the similarity of these views to the above-mentioned models of democracy and public space. According to Krouse (1982: 511), it is possible to distinguish among three broad orientations within democratic theory: radical (or neo-Rousseauean) theories of participatory democracy, inclining to a delegate or mandate concept of representation; conservative (or neo-Burkean) theories of elite democracy, inclining to a trustee conception; and liberal theories of representative democracy, which seek a more balanced reconciliation of elite competence and mass participation. Such liberal theories embrace representation as a desirable means of promoting [elite, author's note] leadership (or economizing upon time and effort); yet at the same time seek to preserve effective political equality and popular sovereignty.

Similarly, most modern authors believe that a balance between the delegate and trustee views is best for democracy, because citizens have limited capacities to absorb (and critically process) sufficient amounts of relevant information in order to direct their "instructions" to elected representatives. As demonstrated by empirical research, individuals (policy makers) respond to public opinion in specific ways, according to their own views of the public's role in decision making, and these views are not always ideally balanced (Foyle 1999). This was studied in the Czech Republic by Brokl, Mansfeldová & Seidlová (2001). While these authors identified some ambivalence in the views of Members of the Chamber of Deputies, there was a general tendency towards balance between the two views:

> While Deputies of one type feel bound by their conscience only ("Trustee"), another type feel bound by their voters ("Delegate") and are ready to obey even if there is a conflict of conscience. Deputies of a third type, which is more characteristic for European countries, find themselves in between the above two types, trying to respect circumstances without losing face when making decisions (ibid: 304).

Authors of the above study depart from the modern theoretical concept of **accountability:**

> As yet, the concept is not entirely free of speculation, but it gives us a satisfactory interpretative framework for the multiple relationships and processes going on between citizens (voters) and politicians, amongst politicians, and between political institutions and elites in general. ... The concept of accountability includes elements of monitoring and supervision, finding and taking account of facts, on one hand, and continues in the enlightenment's project of submitting power to law and justification.

Accountability is the antithesis of power monologue. It establishes a dialogue between responsible actors, on one hand, and supervising actors, sovereigns, i.e. citizens, on the other hand. Both sides are obliged to get involved in public debate (ibid: 299–300).

We have thus, after taking a detour, returned to the thesis that the nature of mutual relations is to a great extent determined by mutual dependency that ties different actors together in their social lives. Clearly, even in representative party democracies, citizens' interests are identified and expressed through continuous elite-public interaction as well as through the different election cycles (at different elections levels), and therefore, the election act is rather a climax, a concentrated outcome of mutual communication. Do elites and the general public trust each other? And what ways of communication (and participation) are deemed legitimate? Based on the above, we can also ask the question whether elites influence the public or vice versa. Finding answers to these questions may help us clarify the elite-public relationship and the distribution of power in a given society.

Once again, we will frame our empirical analysis by the concept of political support, and more specifically, the last dimension thereof, political disaffection. This is defined by Di Palma (1970: 30) as "the subjective feeling of powerlessness, cynicism and lack of confidence in the political process, politicians and democratic institutions, but with no questioning of the political regime." Torcal & Montero (2006) further distinguish between **political disengagement** and **institutional disaffection**. The former is a set of attitudes related to the lack of participation in the political process and a general lack of trust of politics. The latter comprises of beliefs about (the lack of) accountability in political authorities and institutions and a lack of trust therein.

Institutional disaffection

For the purposes of our publication, we understand the concept of institutional disaffection in the broadest sense as the ways people evaluate (not only) elites and their relationship with the general public. Among the key aspects appear existing levels of trust in political institutions, their representatives, and their ability to rule responsibly and lead the public. Low trust of political authorities is frequently mentioned by the media and perceived as a source of low legitimacy of political figures as well as their decisions, laws, and the country's political system as

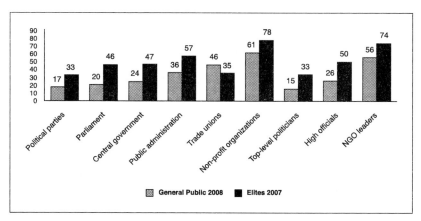

Figure 5.5: Trust in institutions and representatives thereof (per cent)
Sources: CESES 2007, 2008.
Note: Values represent the percentages of respondents who strongly trust or rather trust.

a whole. The cyclical nature of trust, with high levels of trust in new governments gradually diminishing over the time they have been in office, is common to practically all contemporary European democracies. The replacement of little trusted politicians by new ones enjoying higher public trust, at least after taking office, is part of the natural order of democratic politics (Dalton 1998). Many political support scholars point out that trust in individuals is the most specific and short-lasting of all types of political support. In spite of that, a more detailed study of the elite-public relationship is essential for two reasons. First, this relationship plays a key role in democratic theory and political support, and second, there is a clear shift towards more individualized (perhaps more specifically, personified) politics, the weaker role of political parties (Dalton & Wattenberg 2000), and a weaker relationship between election behavior and voters' social position (Franklin, Mackie & Valen 1992). Numerous examples demonstrate that modern politics is increasingly oriented on individual candidates, rather than political parties, even in party systems (Wattenberg 1991, Bean 1993).[66] Short-term factors such as a politician's image, media coverage, and personal life are becoming important for countries' orientations. Such personification of politics can be found in the Czech Republic as well, as exemplified by figures

---

66 E.g. Perot in the United States, Berlusconi in Italy, Haider in Austria, and Fico in Slovakia.

such as Vladimír Železný or Jana Bobošíková. Also characteristic is the fact that "independent candidates" frequently penetrate higher level politics, a domain that used to belong to traditional political parties.

While members of the general public clearly tend to express little trust in political institutions and authorities (e.g. relative to trade unions, non-profit organizations, or their leaders), almost half of elite respondents trust the public administration, central government, and the Parliament. Even the group of actors with the least public trust — political parties and politicians themselves — earn trust in one-third of elites (as opposed to less than one-fifth of the general public). Among elites, ODS and KDU-ČSL voters trust political institutions the most, while KSČM voters trust them the least. ČSSD voters, other party voters, and non-voters express little trust as well. Party winners tend to give more trust not only to "their own" government but also to political parties and the Parliament, with the exception of Green party voters, who are generally more critical than those of the other two coalition parties. Political elites also express more trust in political institutions. Administrative and security elites tend to trust the public administration.[67]

Similar party winner-loser differences in trust in political institutions and authorities can be found in the general public. Practically all cases show significantly different levels of trust between party winners and losers. Party winners as well as people with higher ISEI tend to trust more. ODS voters are a group where trust in political parties and politicians is shared by elites and the general public alike (34% and 33%, respectively).

Since intra-elite differences in levels of trust are relatively minor, we are able to conclude that, despite the above differences on governance forms and ratings of current situation, Czech elites agree on one thing: their view of themselves. Not only do they perceive and rate their own role in society much more positively than the general public, which is little surprising, but they also agree on such rating amongst themselves.

An overwhelming majority of elites disagree with the view that the development of society has gone out of "their" control. The risk of a corrupt symbiosis between politicians and businesses is also found unrealistic. In contrast, half of respondents are convinced that elites are responsible in that they are focusing on solving substantial problems. These majority attitudes are mostly not shared by KSČM voters as well as civic and cultural elites, but the relationship is rather weak.

---

67   See Chapter 2 for detailed analysis of intra-elite trust.

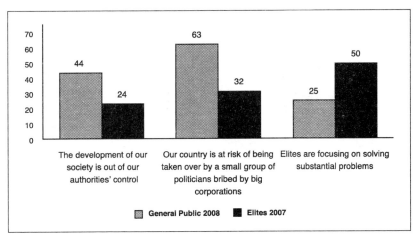

Figure 5.6: Accountability of political institutions and authorities or the lack thereof (per cent)
Sources: CESES 2007, 2008.

Similarly, most of the general public agrees on their view of elites, yet this view is a negative one. The general public is much more critical of elites. ODS voters and people with the highest ISEI, as the only exceptions, are slightly more approving of elites, but even these groups are very critical and, in their views, distant from elites themselves. Other party voters and people with the lowest ISEI do not find Czech elites accountable vis-à-vis their voters or, more generally, their country. Indeed, they see elites as corrupt groups that are not solving real problems (and would be incapable even if they wanted to).

Practically all normative theories of democracy find the following aspects of the elite-public relationship key: the extent to which the general public is able to control its elites, the extent to which access to the elite is closed to non-elites (upward mobility), and the extent to which elites pursue public interest (i.e. whether they are accountable and take public opinion into consideration).

From this perspective, the Czech general public views elites as a relatively hostile and closed group of people manipulating public opinion. Elites "massage", manage, and manipulate public opinion in order to earn support for their decisions (Rounce 2004). Not only political elites, but also economic elites and other interest groups take part in this manipulation, e.g. through financing various associations,

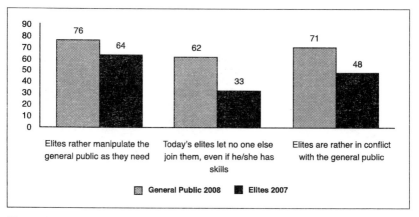

Figure 5.7: The elite-public relationship (per cent)

Sources: CESES 2007, 2008.

Note: A battery of three pairs of competing statements was read out and for each pair, respondents were asked to choose one preferred statement. The figure depicts only the percentages of respondents who strongly agreed or rather agreed with the second statement in each pair.

think-tanks, research institutions, or media campaigns (Manza & Cook 2002). Theories of power inform us that manipulation is the most effective power instrument for asserting one's interests and, combined with elites' relative closedness, contributes to the feelings of disempowerment vis-à-vis the ruling elites. This perceived disempowerment is confirmed by other surveys focusing on citizens' influence at different levels of decision making (local and central) as well as our findings about the ways the general public sees itself as a political actor (see below). It is typical that the statement about manipulating the general public is also largely supported by elites themselves, being one of the few attitudes Czech elites and public agree on.

Political disengagement

Does the low political support for political authorities indicate a threat to democracy or rather a transition towards the postmodern "critical citizenship"? As we suggested above, support for participative democracy may be a mere declaration, since it does not correspond to the Czech general public's other attitudes, which at times sharply contradict some democratic principles. It is also important how the Czech general public views itself as a political actor and rates its own ability to understand and influence society's actions and orientations. Does the general public constitute an important actor in the political system, or is it rather politically disengaged, unable to take an active part in managing public affairs and control its elites? And is this self-depiction of the general public coherent with the way it is viewed by elites?

The Czech general public's strongly critical attitudes towards political parties are complemented by the low frequency of positive attitudes such as identification with political parties. Political science tends to see such identification as one of the principal factors of public support for political parties, the party system, and the political order these parties work in. It is assumed that people declaring party identification also tend to support the existing political system and its institutions (elections and political parties in general), more than those without identification (Miller & Listhaug 1990; Holmberg 2003). Therefore, declining party identification in Western Europe is viewed as a sign of political parties' weakening position in the system of interest representation and a related falling support for representative party democracy (Dalton 1999, Holmberg 2003). Low political support may change the nature of the political system, its election rules, and political behavior. The election behavior of voters who are less emotionally bound to a political party tends to be more volatile, and elites may respond to skeptical voters by

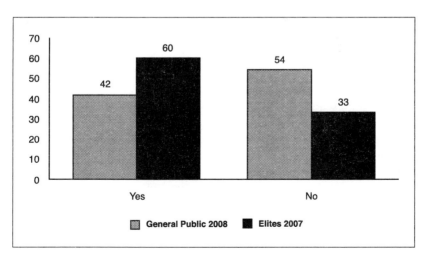

Figure 5.8: Is there a political party you find yourself closer to than other parties? Sources: CESES 2007, 2008.

populism, party fragmentation, or creating new parties that are bound to lose support as quickly as they received it. Ulrich Beck (1996) and other authors conclude that political issues become increasingly absent from the traditional political channels, including political parties.

The Czech general public declares a greater distance from political parties than elites. Levels of party identification are little diversified. While KSČM voters declare the highest level of identification (77%), other parliamentary parties have strongly identified voters as well (75% KDU-ČSL, 69% ODS, and 63% ČSSD). The Green Party is the only exception, with only 39% of identifiers. Other party voters and, above all, non-voters (3%) declare the lowest levels of identification. Therefore, the concern (e.g. Paskeviciute 2006) that political party identification cannot be read as an indicator of democratic support in post-communist countries — because such support is mostly addressed to parties working towards a partial or full regime change — does not seem to apply anymore. While the Communist party clearly has the most identified voters, such identification has also emerged in other parties' electorates, and thus is not exclusive to the KSČM. This finding is further supported by the fact that the relationship with socio-economic status is not statistically significant.

General public as a political actor

The issue of political competence has traditionally been in the center of European political thought.[68] Early conceptions of the so-called civic virtues can be found in classic Greek philosophy. Modern political philosophy distinguishes between two schools of thought about the moral and political qualities of a good democratic citizen: the liberal politics and the republican politics (Burtt 1993). Since we cannot deal with the differences between both schools in detail, we will further emphasize their common aspects in terms of civic political competence in democracy, which, given the orientation of our study, will be further generalized as reflection of ongoing modernization changes. As noted by Warren (2000), "the list of potential civic virtues is a long one: attentiveness to the common good and concerns for justice; tolerance of the views of others; trustworthiness; willingness to participate, deliberate, and listen; respect for the rule of law; and respect for the rights of others" (ibid. 73). Orientation in ongoing social changes is another important aspect of our generalized approach to competencies of the general public as a political actor.

---

68 Some similarities can be found in Confucianism and its public ethics.

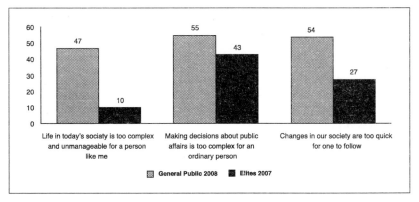

Figure 5.9: Orientation in ongoing social changes and public affairs (per cent)
Sources: CESES 2007, 2008.
Note: Values represent the percentages of respondents who strongly agree or rather agree.

About half the general public respondents feel more or less disoriented and find life in today's society too complex and difficult to manage. It is the level of disorientation that strongly separates the general public. ODS voters and people with higher socio-economic status tend to feel the best oriented. The lower one's status, the worse their perceived disorientation is. In contrast, elites feel "at home" in today's society and most of them doubt that an ordinary person can understand political decision making in sufficient detail. This does not only demonstrate Czech elites' leadership deficit (Frič et al. 2008), but also their mistrust in the general public's real ability to play the role of active political actors, as required by the most preferred participative model of democracy.

Table 5.6: Evaluations of the general public as a political actor

		GP08/E07	GP08/E07	
1	They are rather fearful, afraid to speak out publicly	60/59%	35/38%	They are rather proud and are not afraid to speak out publicly
2	They usually quarrel when it comes to public affairs	63/66%	32/31%	They usually play for the team
3	Despite some complaining, they eventually do what elites want them to do	64/67%	30/29%	They eventually do what they want, no matter what elites want

Sources: CESES 2007, 2008.
Note: Don't knows add up to 100%.

In a rare agreement, elites and the general public perceive people in the Czech Republic as fearful, quarreling followers of their elites. This only further strengthens people's reliance on elites and their ability to change the situation. The ways of political and, more generally, social change that are preferred by Czech society are in sharp contrast both with its strict refusal of trustee democracy and the principles of representative democracy as based on political parties competing in a marketplace of visions and ideas.

5.4 Conclusion

Let us now attempt to answer the questions we posed in the beginning of this chapter. First, we can clearly conclude that support for democracy as a political regime is high in the Czech Republic, both among the general public and, even higher, among elites. A relatively small percentage of people rate the current democratic regime negatively when compared to the prior regime, and democracy really is "the only game in town" to most people. The second clear conclusion is that while both actors prefer the participative model of democracy, they place different emphases on public participation. Elites lean towards a balance between representative and participative elements, while the general public strongly supports direct democracy. Given that information, democracy and its institutions might seem to be functioning rather smoothly in the Czech Republic. However, a different picture appears when we assume the relational perspective, taking democracy as a system of power distribution and sharing between elites and the general public. Although constitutional institutions now build upon a solid foundation of the political system and democracy is generally acknowledged as the best form of government, some aspects of the elite-public relationship might, in our opinion, jeopardize the democratic character of the country's political system in future.

Above all, there is a relatively large group of people we call critical non-democrats, who are discontent with existing political regime and its current development, and simultaneously express anti-democratic attitudes. Almost one-third of the Czech general public is willing to sacrifice democratic principles for more security, order, and prosperity. These people agree that Parliament be resolved and a strong leader take power. Moreover, 25% of them want to change the regime in our society radically, through revolution. In the latter case, an optimist would argue that a revolutionary change might be supported by non-democrats as well as those democrats and intellectuals who are too critical of the ways democracy is currently working and see revolution as the only means to improve democracy. However, our data does not support this optimistic hypothesis. Indeed, people respecting democratic principles and those with higher socio-economic status tend to view the public's performance as a political actor more critically and are less excited about direct democracy.

Another important finding is that democrats are disgusted with the current course of events and call for a more consensual politics. This can take the form of shared left-right rule, one that is expected by the general public to solve essential long-term problems such as pension and health care reforms, despite all risks such a form of rule entails (see above). Almost half of the population also support the idea of a strong leader who would overcome endless parliamentary squabbles and define a clear future orientation for the country. At least some part of these respondents likely see such a leader as a personality capable of defining the country's strategic interests and pursuing them through specific policies, rather than an undemocratic, authoritative ruler. People are not primarily disgusted by the mistakes individual parties and their representatives have made, or their political programs they can either agree or disagree with. Most people probably understand the fact that political dispute belongs to democracy, making it easier for them to decide who to vote for. What really disgusts them in politics is the style political disputes are waged by Czech elites. They are tired of the endless mobilization of one group against another and repeated warnings of the immense threat to democracy, our national interest, or "ordinary people" that a given enemy party poses. People usually do not think within these categories and, moreover, elites cannot fulfill people's expectations by playing these games. Therefore, calls for both camps to form grand coalitions or technocratic governments are hardly surprising because they offer prospects of a temporary truce and a relief from the permanent political squabble. Herein is a risk that a mostly democratic part of the general public would favor reducing the role of political parties in governance and, within the political system, reducing their role in formulating, aggregating, and advocating group interests and in the competition between candidates for voter support.

This brings us to the last aspect of the elite-public relationship, i.e. the lack of mutual respect. The Czech general public does not trust its elites and any expectations it may hold are certainly not being fulfilled by existing elites. Similarly, elites do not find the general public to be a fitting partner in sharing power and are sure that the public is easily manipulated. They act correspondingly, suggesting they can do anything without being stopped — from intervening in the justice system to insulting their competitors, to manipulating public procurement. This skeptical view of the general public is shared by a large part of the public itself, and therefore, we cannot describe Czechs as actors who respect democratic principles and find intrinsic value in democracy. Their preference of greater civic responsibility for governance and their critical view of ruling elites are, therefore, a mere rhetoric rather than a sign of social modernization as we know it from Western Europe. The Czech general public does not feel equal partners with its elites. It rather expects elites to abuse their powers, and what is more, does not feel capable of stopping them. This may be the source of beliefs that only a strong leader can protect public interest from the corrupt elites. Also related to people's low confidence in their own political competence is their continuing reliance on the government and public assistance.

References

Almond, G. – Verba, S. 1963. *The Civic Culture*. Princeton: Princeton University Press.

Anderson, C. J. – Guillory, C. A. 1997. Political institutions and satisfaction with democracy: A cross-national analysis of consensus and majoritarian systems. *American Political Science Review* 91 (1): 66–81.

Anderson, C. J. – Tverdova, Y. V. 2001. Winners, losers, and attitudes about government in contemporary democracies. *International Political Science Review* 22 (4): 321–338.

Antonakis, J. – Atwater, L. 2002. Leader Distance: A Review and a Proposed Theory. *Leadership Quarterly* 13 (6): 673–704.

Antonakis, J. 2006. Leadership: What is it and how it is implicated in strategic management? *International Journal of Management Cases* 8 (4): 4–20.

Aron, R. 1950. Social Structure and the Ruling Class. *British Journal of Sociology* 1 (2): 1–17 and 126–144.

Aron, R. 1968. The Promethean Dream: Society in Search of Itself. In *Britannica Perspectives*. Vol. II. Chicago: Encyclopaedia Britannica. Pp. 5–235.

Bachrach, P. 1969. *The Theory of Democratic Elitism*. London: University of London Press.

Baker, W. E. 1994. *Networking Smart: How to Build Relationships for Personal and Organizational Success*. New York: McGraw-Hill.

Barber, B. R. 1984. *Strong Democracy: Participatory Politics for a New Age*. University of California Press: Berkeley.

Bean, C. 1993. The electoral influence of party leader images in Australia and New Zealand. *Comparative Political Studies* 26 (1): 111–132.

Beck, U. 1996. World Risk Society as Cosmopolitan Society? Ecological Questions in a Framework of Manufactured Uncertainties. *Theory, Culture & Society* 13 (4): 1–32.

Bennis, W. – Nanus, B. 1985. *Leaders: The Strategies for Taking Charge*. New York: Harper and Row.

Bessette, J. 1980. Deliberative Democracy: The Majority Principle in Republican Government. In *How Democratic is the Constitution?*, edited by R. A. Goldwin – W. A. Schambra. Washington, D.C.: AEI Press. Pp. 102–116.

Bessette, J. 1994. *The Mild Voice of Reason.* University of Chicago Press: Chicago.

Bowen, L. 1974. Almost Everything You Ever Wanted to Know About Leadership. *Fortune* 80: 241–242.

Brokl, L. – Mansfeldová, Z. – Seidlová, A. 2001. Vztah poslanců českého parlamentu k voličům jako problém vertikální odpovědnosti [The Relationship of Members of the Czech Parliament to Voters as a Matter of Vertical Accountability]. *Sociologický časopis / Czech Sociological Review* 37 (3): 297–311.

Burns, M. J. 1978. *Leadership.* New York: Harper & Row.

Burton, M. – Higley, J. 1998. Political Crises and Elite Settlements. In *Elites, Crises, and the Origins of Regimes*, edited by M. Dogan – J. Higley. Lanham, MD: Rowman & Littlefield Publishers. Pp. 44–70.

Burtt, S. 1993. The Politics of Virtue Today: A Critique and a Proposal. *The American Political Science Review* 87 (2): 360–368.

Co si myslíte o české politické scéně? [What do you think of the Czech political scene?] 2007. *DNES* 13 November 2007: 6.

COLLINSON, D. L. 2005. Questions of distance. *Leadership* 1(2): 235–250.

Crozier, M. – Huntington, S. P. – Watanuki, J. 1975. *The Crisis of Democracy: Report on the Governability of Democracies to the Trilateral Commission.* New York: New York University.

CVVM. 2004. *Přínos zemí Visegrádské čtyřky Evropě* [The contribution of the Visegrad Four countries to Europe]. Prague: Public Opinion Research Centre of the Czech Academy of Sciences (CVVM).

Dahl, R. A. 1961. *Who Governs?* New Haven: Yale University Press.

Dahrendorf, R. 1994. Svoboda a sociální vazby. Poznámky ke struktuře argumentace [Freedom and social ties: Notes on the structure of argument]. In *Liberální společnost* [Liberal society], edited by M. Znoj. Prague: Filosofia. Pp. 9–16.

Dalton, R. – Bürklin, W. – Drummond, A. 2001. Public opinion and direct democracy. *Journal of Democracy* 12 (4): 141–153.

Dalton, R. 1996. *Citizen Politics: Public Opinion and Political Parties in Advanced Industrial Democracies.* Chatham: Chatham House.

Dalton, R. 1998. *Political Support in Advanced Industrial Democracies.* Irvine, CA: Center for the Study of Democracy. CSD Paper 98–01.

Dalton, R. 1999. Political Support in Advanced Industrial Democracies. In *Critical Citizens: Global Support for Democratic Government*, edited by P. Norris. Oxford: Oxford University Press. Pp. 57–77.

Dalton, R. 2000. Citizen Attitudes and Political Behavior. *Comparative Political Studies* 33 (6/7): 912–940.

Dalton, R. 2004. *Democratic Challenges, Democratic Choices: The Erosion of Political Support in Advanced Industrial Democracies.* Oxford: Oxford University Press.

Di Palma, G. 1970. *Apathy and Participation. Mass Politics in Western Societies.* New York: The Free Press.

Diamond, L. 1999. *Developing democracy: Toward consolidation.* Baltimore: Johns Hopkins University Press.

diZerega, G. 1991. Elites and Democratic Theory. *The Review of Politics* 53 (2): 340–372.

Dogan, M. 2003. Introduction: Diversity of Elite Configurations and Clusters of Power. In *Elite Configurations at the Apex of Power,* edited by M. Dogan. Leiden: Brill.

Domhoff, W. G. 1967. *Who Rules America?* Englewood Cliffs: Prentice Hall.

Dowding, K. 2008. Perceptions of Leadership [online]. In *Public Leadership: Perspectives and Practices,* edited by P. 't Hart – J. Uhr. Canberra: Australian National University E Press. Pp. 93–102. http://epress.anu.edu.au/anzsog/public_leadership/pdf/whole_book.pdf

Dvořáková, V. – Kunc, J. 1994. *O přechodech k demokracii* [On democratic transitions]. Prague: SLON.

Easton, D. 1975. A Re-Assessment of the Concept of Political Support. *British Journal of Political Science* 5: 453–457.

Easton, D. 1979. *A Systems Analysis of Political Life.* Chicago: University of Chicago Press.

Edinger, L. J. 1975. The Comparative Analysis of Political Leadership. *Comparative Politics* 7 (2): 253–269.

Eldersveld, S. 1989. *Political Elites in Modern Societies: Empirical Research and Democratic Theory.* Ann Arbor: University of Michigan Press.

Etzioni-Halevy, E. 1990. The Relative Autonomy of Élites: The Absorption of Protest and Social Progress in Western Democracies. In *Rethinking Progress,* edited by J. C. Alexander – P. Sztompka. Boston: Unwin Hyman. Pp. 202–226.

Etzioni-Halevy, E. 1993. *The Elite Connection: Problems and Potential of Western Democracy.* Cambridge: Polity Press.

Ferree, M. M. et al. 2002. Four models of the public sphere in modern democracies. *Theory and Society* 31: 289–324.

Field, L. G. – Higley, J. – Burton, M. 1990. A New Elite Framework for Political Sociology. *Revue Européene des Sciences Sociales* 28: 149–182.

Field, L. G. – Higley, J. 1980. *Elitism.* London: Routledge & Kegan Paul.

Foyle, D. C. 1999. *Counting the Public In: Presidents, Public Opinion, and Foreign Policy.* New York: Columbia University Press.

Franklin, M. – Mackie, T. – Valen, H. (eds.) 1992. *Electoral change: Response to evolving social and attitudinal structures in western countries.* Cambridge University Press: New York.

Freud, S. 1996. *Psychológia masy a analýza Ja* [Group psychology and the analysis of the ego]. Bratislava: Archa. Originally published 1923.

Frič, P. – Nekola, M. – Prudký, L. 2005. *Elity a modernizace* [Elites and Modernization]. Prague: Center for Social and Economic Strategies, Faculty of Social Sciences, Charles University in Prague. CESES Papers No. 1/2005. http://www.ceses.cuni.cz/CESES-20-version1-sesit05_01_fric.pdf

Frič, P. 2003. Modernizační strategie obyvatelstva [The population's modernization strategies]. In Češi na cestě za svojí budoucností: Budoucnost a modernizace v postojích a očekáváních obyvatelstva [Czechs on their way into the future: The future and modernization in people's attitudes and expectations], edited by P. Frič. Prague: G plus G.

Frič, P. 2005. Strategie modernizace ČR: komparace názorů elit a veřejnosti [Modernization strategies for the Czech Republic: Comparing elite and public opinions]. In *Elity a modernizace: Průběžná zpráva z výzkumu* [Elites and modernization: Interim research report], edited by P. Frič – M. Nekola – L. Prudký. Prague: Center for Social and Economic Strategies, Faculty of Social Sciences, Charles University in Prague. Pp. 13-29. CESES Papers No. 1/2005. http://www.ceses.cuni.cz/CESES-20-version1-sesit05_01_fric.pdf

Frič, P. 2007. *Neformální sítě: Situace v České republice z pohledu českých elit* [Informal networks: Situation in the Czech Republic from the elite perspective]. Prague: GfK.

Frič, P. 2008. Konspirační teorie: Jak vznikají, jakou mají strukturu a proč jim věříme? [Conspiracy theories: How they arise, what structure they have, and why we believe them.] Prague: GfK.

Frič, P. et al. 2003. *Češi na cestě za svojí budoucností* [Czechs on their way into the future]. Prague: G plus G.

Frič, P. et al. 2008. *Vůdcovství českých elit* [Leadership in Czech elites]. Prague: Grada Publishing.

Friedrich, C. J. 1942. *The New Belief in the Common Man*. Boston: Little, Brown.

Fuchs, D. – Guidorossi, G. – Svenson, P. 1995. Support for the Democratic System. In *Citizens and the State*, edited by H.-D. Klingemann – D. Fuchs. New York: Oxford University Press. Pp. 323–353.

Fuchs, D. 1993. Trends of Political Support in the Federal Republic of Germany. In *Political Culture in Germany*, edited by D. Berg-Schlosser – R. Rytlewski. London: Macmillan. Pp. 232–268.

Fukuyama, F. 1992. *The End of History and the Last Man*. New York: Maxwell Macmillan.

Gabriel, Y. 1997. Meeting God: When Organizational Members Come Face to Face with the Supreme Leader. *Human Relations* 50 (4): 315–42.

Gamson, W. A. 1968. *Power and Discontent*. Homewood, IL: The Dorsey Press.

Ganzeboom, H. B. G. – De Graaf, P. – Treiman, D. J. 1992. A Standard International Socio-Economic Index of Occupational Status. *Social Science Research* 21 (1): 1–56.

Giddens, A. 1975. *The Class Structure of the Advanced Societies*. New York: Harper Torchbooks.

Habermas, J. 1984. *The Theory of Communicative Action*. Vol. 1. Cambridge: Polity Press.

Habermas, J. 1990. What Does Socialism Mean Today? The Rectifying Revolution and the Need for New Thinking on the Left. *New Left Review* 183: 3–21.

Havelka, M. – Müller, K. 1999. Institutional Tensions of Radicalized Transformation. An Assessment in the Modernization Perspective. In *System Change and Modernization*, edited by W. Adamski – J. Bunčák – P. Machonin – D. Martin. Warsaw: IfiS Publishers. Pp. 81–93.

Hayward, J. (ed.) 1996. *Élitism, Populism, and European Politics*. Oxford: Clarendon Press.

Higley, J. – Burton, M. 1997. Types of Elites in Postcommunist Eastern Europe. *International Politics* 34: 153–168.

Higley, J. – Lengyel, G. (eds.) 2000. *Elites after State Socialism: Theories and Analysis*. Oxford: Rowman & Littlefield.

Higley, J. – Lengyel, G. 2000. Introduction: Elite Configuration after State Socialism. In *Elites after State Socialism: Theories and Analysis*, edited by J. Higley – G. Lengyel. Oxford: Rowman & Littlefield Publishers. Pp. 1–21.

Higley, J. et al. 1991. Elite integration in stable democracies: a reconsideration. *European Sociological Review* 7 (1): 35–53.

Hloušek, V. – Kopeček, L. 2003. *Demokracie: Teorie, modely, osobnosti, podmínky, nepřátelé a perspektivy demokacie* [Democracy: Theories, models, personalities, conditions, enemies, and perspectives]. Brno: International Institute for Political Studies.

Hofstede, G. 1980. *Culture's Consequences: International Differences in Work-Related Values*. London: SAGE.

Hofstede, G. 2001. *Culture's consequences*. Thousand Oaks, London, New Delhi: Sage Publications.

Hogg, M. A. 2001. A Social Identity Theory of Leadership. *Personality and Social Psychology Review* 5 (3): 184–200.

Hollander, E. P. 1993. Legitimacy, Power, and Influence: A perspective on Relational Features of Leadership. In *Leadership Theory and Research Perspectives and Directions,* edited by M. M. Chemers – R. Ayman. New York: Academic Press. Pp. 29–47.

Holmberg, S. 2003. Are Political Parties Necessary? *Electoral Studies* 22 (2): 287–299.

Holý, L. 2001. *Malý český člověk a skvělý český národ: Národní identita a postkomunistická transformace společnosti* [The little Czech person and the great Czech nation: National identity and the post-communist social transformation]. Prague: SLON.

Hoppe, H.-H. 1992. *Natural Elites, Intellectuals, and the State* [online]. Auburn, AL: Ludwig von Mises Institute. http://www.mises.org/etexts/intellectuals.asp

Huntington, S. P. 1981. *American Politics*. Cambridge, MA: Harvard University Press.

Huntington, S. P. 1991. *The Third Wave*. Norman: University of Oklahoma Press.

Husák, P. 1997. *Budování kapitalismu v Čechách: Rozhovory s Tomášem Ježkem* [Building capitalism in Bohemia: Interviews with Tomáš Ježek]. Prague: Volvox Globator.

Inglehart, R. – Norris, P. 2003. Rising Tide: *Gender Equality and Cultural Change around the World*. Cambridge: Cambridge University Press.

Inglehart, R. (ed.). 2003. *Human Values and Social Change*. Leiden: Brill.

Inglehart, R. 1977. *The Silent Revolution: Changing Values and Political Styles among Western Publics*. Princeton: Princeton University Press.

Inglehart, R. 1997. *Modernization and Postmodernization: Cultural, Economic and Political Change*. Princeton, NJ: Princeton University Press.

Jacobs, J. 2001. *Modernization, core values and the people: Consolidation of political democracy and market economy in Central and Eastern Europe in comparative perspective* [online]. Frankfurt/Oder: European University Viadrina. Policy Paper Series "Democratic Values" No. 6. http://viadrina.euv-frankfurt-o.de/~vgkul-soz/EU%20Projekt/papers/Pp6.pdf

Jenks C. 1997. *Cultura*. London, New York: Routledge.

Joubert, D. 1992. *Reflections on Social Values*. Pretoria: Human Sciences Research Council.

Kaminski, A. Z. – Kurczewska, J. 1995. Strategies of Post-communist Transformations: Elites as Institutions Builders. In *Social Change and Modernization: Lessons from Eastern Europe*, edited by B. Grancelli. Berlin: Walter de Gruytrer. Pp. 131–152.

Kandert, J. 2002. Vznikání nových elit – český případ [Emerging elites: The Czech case]. In *Konsolidace vládnutí a podnikání v České republice a v Evropské unii II* [Consolidation of governance and the business environment in the Czech Republic and the European Union, volume II], edited by J. Končelík – B. Köpplová – I. Prázová. Prague: Matfyzpress. Pp. 82–88.

Keller, J. 2001. *Politika s ručením omezeným: Proměny moci na prahu 21. století* [Politics Ltd.: Changes of power in the wake of the 21st century]. Prague: Evropský literární klub.

Keller, S. I. 1963. *Beyond the Ruling Class: Strategic Elites in Modern Society*. New York: Random House.

Keller, S. I. 1980. *The Social Origins and Career Lines of Three Generations of American Business Leaders*. New York: Arno Press.

Klaus, V. 2004. A transformative visionary. Interviewed by K. McCahon. *Fraser Forum* 10: 21–23.

Klingemann, H.-D. – Fuchs, D. 1995. *Citizens and the State*. Oxford: Oxford University Press.

Klingemann, H.-D. 1998. *Mapping Political Support in the 1990s: A Global Analysis*. Berlin: Wissenschaftszentrum Berlin für Sozialforschung. Discussion Paper FS III 98–202.

Kluckhohn, C. 1967. Values and Value Orientations in the Theory of Action: An Exploration in Definition and Classification. In *Towards a General Theory of Action*, edited by T. Parsons – E. A. Shils. Cambridge, MA: Harvard University Press. Pp. 390–430.

Kornhauser, W. 1960. *The Politics of Mass Society*. New York: The Free Press.

Kouzes, J. M. – Posner, B. Z. 1995. *The Leadership Challenge: How to Keep Getting Extraordinary Things Done in Organizations*. San Francisco: Jossey-Bass Publishers.

Krouse, R. W. 1982. Two Concepts of Democratic Representation: James and John Stuart Mill. *Journal of Politics* 44 (2): 509–537.

Lewin, K. 1935. *A dynamic theory of personality*. New York: McGraw-Hill.

Linde, J. – Ekman, J. 2003. Satisfaction with Democracy: A Note on a Frequently Used Indicator in Comparative Politics. *European Journal of Political Research* 42 (3): 391–408.

Linz, J. J. – Stepan, A. 1996. *Problems of Democratic Transition and Consolidation: Southern Europe, South America, and Post-Communist Europe*. Baltimore: Johns Hopkins University Press.

Lord, R. G. – Brown, D. J. 2001. Leadership, values, and subordinate self-concepts. *Leadership Quarterly* 12: 133–152.

Machačová, J. – Matějček, J. 2002. *Nástin sociálního vývoje českých zemí 1781–1914* [A brief social history of the Czech Lands 1781–1914]. Opava: The Silesia Museum.

Machonin, P. 2000. Teorie modernizace a česká zkušenost [Modernization theory and the Czech experience]. In *Ekonomické a společenské změny v české společnosti po roce 1989* [Economic and social changes in Czech society after 1989], edited by L. Mlčoch – P. Machonin – M. Sojka. Prague: Karolinum. Pp. 97–218.

Machonin, P. et al. 2001. Strukturální změny v postsocialistické České republice a aktuální výzvy modernizace [Structural changes in the post-socialist Czech Republic and current modernization challenges]. In *Transformace a modernizační výzvy* [Transformation and modernization challenges], edited by W. Adamski – P. Machonin – W. Zapf. Prague: Institute of Sociology of the Czech Academy of Sciences. Proceedings from a conference of European sociologists in Prague 2001.

Manza, J. – Cook, F. L. 2002. A Democratic Polity? Three Views of Policy Responsiveness to Public Opinion in the United States. *American Politics Research* 30 (6): 630–667.

McAllister, I. 1991. Party-elites, Voters and Political Attitudes: Testing Three Explanations for Mass-Elite Differences. *Canadian Journal of Political Science* 24 (2): 337–268.

McCrone, D. J. – Kuklinski, J. H. 1979. The Delegate Theory of Representation. *American Journal of Political Science* 23 (2): 278–300.

Meindl, J. R. 1995. The Romance of Leadership as a Follower-Centric Theory: A Social Constructionist Approach. *Leadership Quarterly* 6 (3): 329–341.

Michels, R. 1931. Strany a vůdcové: k sociologii politického stranictví [Zur Soziologie des Parteiwesens in der modernen Demokratie.] Prague: Orbis.

Milén, P. 2002. *Cesta do budověku: Esej o velkých změnách 21. století* [A way into the future age: An essay about the great changes of the 21st century]. Prague: Prostor.

Miller, A. H. – Listhaug, O. 1990. Political Parties and Confidence in Government: A Comparison of Norway, Sweden, and the United States. *British Journal of Political Science* 29 (3): 357–386.

Miller, A. H. 1974. Political Issues and Trust in Government. *American Political Science Review* 68: 951–972.

Mills, C. W. 1966. *Mocenská elita* [The Power Elite]. Prague: Orbis.

Mishler, W. – Rose, R. 1999. Five Years after the Fall: Trajectories of Support for Democracy in Post-Communist Europe. In *Critical Citizens: Global Support for Democratic Government*, edited by P. Norris Oxford: Oxford University Press. Pp. 78–100.

Mishler, W. – Rose, R. 2001. Political Support for Incomplete Democracies: Realist vs. Idealist Theories and Measures. *International Political Science Review* 22 (4): 303–320.

Moore, G. 1979. The Structure of National Elite Network. *American Sociological Review* 44: 673–692.

Mosca, G. 1939. *The Ruling Class* (Elementi di scienza politica). New York: McGraw-Hill.

Muller, E. N. – Jukam, T. O. – Selingson, M. A. 1982. Diffuse Political Support and Antisystem Political Behavior. *American Journal of Political Science* 26: 240–264.

Muller, E. N. – Jukam, T. O. 1977. On the Meaning of Political Support. *American Political Science Review* 71: 1561–1595.

Musil, J. et al. 2004. *Pojetí sociální soudržnosti v soudobé sociologii a politologii* [Conceptions of social cohesion in contemporary sociology and political science]. Prague: Center for Social and Economic Strategies, Faculty of Social Sciences,

Charles University in Prague. CESES Papers No. 2004/9. http://www.ceses. cuni.cz/CESES-20-version1-sesit04_09_musil.pdf

Největší Čech [The Greatest Czech] [online]. 2005. [s. l.]: Wikipedia. http://cs.wikipedia.org/wiki/Největší_Čech

Nicolaou-Smokoviti, L. 2004. Business Leaders' Work Environment and Leadership Styles. *Current Sociology* 52 (3): 407–427.

Norris, P. (ed.) 1999. *Critical Citizens: Global Support for Democratic Government.* Oxford: Oxford University Press.

Nye, J. S. 1997. *Why people don't trust government.* Cambridge: Harvard University Press.

O'Donnell, G. – Schmitter, P. C. 1986. *Transitions from Authoritarian Rule: Tentative Conclusions about Uncertain Democracies.* Baltimore: John Hopkins University Press.

Olson, M. 1965. *The Logic of Collective Action: A Theory of Interest Groups in Public Goods.* Cambridge: Harvard University Press.

Ortega y Gasset, J. 1969. *Úkol naší doby* [The modern theme]. Prague: Mladá fronta.

Pakulski, J. – Kullberg, J. S. – Higley, J. 1996. The Persistence of Postcommunist Elites. *Journal of Democracy* 7 (2): 133–147.

Palacký, F. 1912. *Poslední mé slovo* [My last word]. Prague: Josef Pelc.

Pareto, V. 1966. *Sociological Writings.* Selected and introduced by A. E. Finer. New York: Pall Mall Press.

Pareto, V. 1968. *The Rise and Fall of the Elites. An Application of Theoretical Sociology.* Totowa, NJ: Bedminster Press.

Parsons, T. 1951. *The Social System.* New York: Free Press.

Paskeviciute, A. 2006. Party Identification and System Legitimacy in Established and New Democracies. In *European Consortium for Political Research (ECPR) Joint Sessions.* Nicosia, Cyprus.

Patočka, J. 1992. *Co jsou Češi? Malý přehled fakt a pokus o vysvětlení* [What are Czechs like? A brief summary of facts and an attempt for explanation]. Prague: Panorama.

Pehe, J. 1996. Český provincialismus [Czech provincialism]. *Nová Přítomnost* 2 (1).

Pehe, J. 1998. České plebejství jako politický problém [Czech plebeian nature as a political problem]. *MF Dnes* 14 December 1998. http://www.pehe.cz/clanky/1998/ceske-plebejstvi-jako-politicky-problem

Pierre, J. – Peters, G. B. 2000. *Governance, Politics and the State.* Houndsmill: Macmillan.

Pirages, D. 1976. *Managing political conflict.* New York: Praeger.

Pitkin, H. F. 1967. *The concept of representation.* Berkeley: University of California Press.

Pollack, D. et al. 2001. *Political culture in post-communist Europe. Attitudes in new democracies: state of the art –theoretical thoughts and ideas* [online]. Frankfurt/Oder: European University Viadrina. Policy Paper Series "Democratic Values" No. 1. http://viadrina.euv-frankfurt-o.de/~vgkulsoz/EU%20Projekt/papers/Pp1neu. pdf

Potůček, M. (ed.) 2002. *Průvodce krajinou priorit pro Českou republiku* [A guide through the landscape of priorities for the Czech Republic]. Prague: Gutenberg. http://ceses.cuni.cz/CESES-34-version1-pruvodce.pdf

Prudký L. 2006. *Přístupy k sociologickému empirickému zkoumání hodnot* [Approaches to the sociological empirical study of values]. Prague: Center for Social and Economic Strategies, Faculty of Social Sciences, Charles University in Prague. CESES Papers No. 4/2006. http://www.ceses.cuni.cz/CESES-20-version1-sesit_06_04.pdf

Prudký, L. et al. 2001. *Religion und Kirchen in Ost (Mittel) Europa: Tschechien, Kroatien, Polen.* Ostfildern: Schwabenverlag.

Prudký, L. et al. 2009. *Inventura hodnot* [Taking inventory of values]. Prague: Academia.

Putnam, R. 1995. Bowling Alone. *Journal of Democracy* 6 (1): 65–78.

Rabušic, L. (ed.) 2001. *Sociální studia.* Vol. 1, no. 6, "České hodnoty 1991–1999" [Czech values 1991-1999]. Brno: Faculty of Social Studies, Masaryk University.

Reicher, S. D. – Haslam, A. S. – Hopkins, N. 2005. Social identity and the dynamics of leadership: Categorization, entrepreneurship and power in the transformation of social reality. *Leadership Quarterly* 16: 547–568.

Remmer, K. L. 1991. The political impact of economic crisis in Latin America in the 1980s. *American Political Science Review* 85 (3): 777–800.

Riesman, D. 1961. *The Lonely Crowd.* New Haven: Yale University Press.

Riker, W. H. 1982. *Liberalism against Populism: A Confrontation between the Theory of Democracy and the Theory of Social Choice.* San Francisco: Freeman.

Rokeach, M. 1967. *Value Survey.* Sunnyvale, CA: Halgren Tests.

Rose, R. – Mishler, W. – Haerpfer, C. 1998. *Democracy and its Alternatives.* Baltimore: Johns Hopkins University Press.

Rost, J. C. 1993. *Leadership for the Twenty-First Century.* Westport, CT: Praeger Publishers.

Rost, J. C. 1995. Leadership: A discussion about ethics. *Business Ethics Quarterly* 5 (1): 129–142.

Rounce, A. D. 2004. Political Actors' Perception of Public Opinion: Assessing the Impact of Opinion on Decision Making [online]. Ottawa: Carleton University. http://www.cpsa-acsp.ca/papers-2004/Rounce.pdf

Ruostetsaari, I. 2006. Social Upheaval and Transformation of Elite Structures: The Case of Finland. *Political Studies* 54: 23–42.

Sartori, G. 1993. *Teória demokracie* [Democratic theory]. Bratislava: Archa.

Schopflin, G. 1991. Post-Communism: Constructing New Democracies in Central Europe. *International Affairs* 67: 235–250.

Schumpeter, J. A. 1942. *Capitalism, Socialism and Democracy*. New York: Harper & Row.

Schwartz, S. H. 1992. Universals in the Content and Structure of Values: Theoretical Advances and Empirical Tests in 20 Countires. *Advances in Experimental Social Psychology* 25: 1–65.

Schwarz, S. – Huismans, S. 1995. Value Priorities in Four Western Religions. *Social Psychology Quarterly* 58: 88–107.

Sinclair, A. 2008. Bodies and Identities in the Construction of Leadership Capital [online]. In *Public Leadership: Perspectives and Practices*, edited by P. 't Hart – J. Uhr. Canberra: Australian National University E Press. Pp. 83–92. http:// epress.anu.edu.au/anzsog/public_leadership/pdf/whole_book.pdf

Slejška, D. et al. 1990. *Sondy do veřejného mínění* [Public opinion surveys]. Prague: Nakladatelství Svoboda.

Stanley, T. J. 1993. *Networking With the Affluent and Their Advisors*. Homewood, IL: Irwin.

Steelman, T. A. 2001. Elite and Participatory Policymaking: Finding Balance in a Case of National Forest Planning. *Policy Studies Journal* 29 (1): 71–89.

Steen, A. 2001. The Question of Legitimacy: Elites and Political Support in Russia. *Europe-Asia Studies* 53 (5): 697–718.

Stogdill, R. M. 1974. *Handbook of Leadership: A Survey of Theory and Research*. New York: The Free Press.

Stout, L. 2006. *Ideal Leadership: Time for a Change*. Shippensburg: Destiny Image Publishing.

Svátek, F. 1993. Poznámky o egalitářství a elitismu v české historické tradici [Notes on egalitarianism and elitism in the Czech historic tradition]. In *Politická a ekonomická transformace v zemích střední a východní Evropy* [Political and economic transformation in Central and Eastern European countries]. Prague: CEFRES.

Terry, R. W. 1993. *Authentic Leadership*. San Francisco: Jossey-Bass.

Thomassen, J. 1995. Support for democratic Values. In *Citizen and the State*, edited by H. Klingemann – D. Fuchs. Oxford: Oxford University Press.

Torcal, M. – Montero, J. R. (Eds.) 2006. *Political disaffection in contemporary democracies: social capital, institutions, and politics*. London: Routledge.

Torcal, M. et al. 2005. *Democratic Support and the Consolidating Effect in New Democracies*. Unpublished manuscript.

Tucker, R. 1981. *Politics and Leadership*. Columbia: University of Missouri Press.

Uhl-Bien, M. – Graen, G. B. – Scandura, T. A. 2000. Implications of Leader-Member Exchange (Lmx) For Strategic Human Resource Management

Systems: Relationships as Social Capital for Competitive Advantage. *Research in Personal and Human Resources Management* 18: 137–185.

Useem, M. 1984. *The inner circle: Large corporations and the rise of business political activity in the US and UK.* New York: Oxford University Press.

van Deth, J. W. – Scarbrough, E. 1995. The Concept of Values. In *The Impact of Values,* edited by J. W. van Deth – E. Scarbrough. Oxford: Oxford University Press. Pp. 21–47.

van Deth, J. W. 1995. Introduction: The Impact of Values. In *The Impact of Values,* edited by J. W. van Deth – E. Scarbrough. Oxford: Oxford University Press. Pp. 1–18.

Warren, M. E. 2000. *Democracy and Association.* Princeton: Princeton University Press.

Wasilewski, J. 2001. Three Elites of the Central/East European Democratization. In *Transformative Paths in Central and Eastern Europe,* edited by R. Markowski – E. Wnuk–Lipiński. Warsaw: Institute of Political Studies, Polish Academy of Sciences. Pp. 133–142.

Wattenberg, M. P. 1991. *The Rise of Candidate Centered Politics.* Cambridge: Harvard University Press.

Datasets

Aufbruch/New Departures [database file]. 1997/8. Vienna: Pastorale Forum in Wien.

Elites in the Czech society [database file]. 2003. Prague: Center for Social and Economic Strategies, Faculty of Social Sciences, Charles University.

Elites in the Czech society [database file]. 2005. Prague: Center for Social and Economic Strategies, Faculty of Social Sciences, Charles University.

European Values Study [database file]. 1991. Cologne: GESIS – Leibniz Institute for the Social Sciences.

European Values Study [database file]. 1999. Cologne: GESIS – Leibniz Institute for the Social Sciences.

General Public as a Modernization Actor I [database file]. 2003. Prague: Center for Social and Economic Strategies, Faculty of Social Sciences, Charles University.

General Public as a Modernization Actor II [database file]. 2005. Prague: Center for Social and Economic Strategies, Faculty of Social Sciences, Charles University.

General Public as a Modernization Actor III [database file]. 2007. Prague: Center for Social and Economic Strategies, Faculty of Social Sciences, Charles University.

ISSP Leisure Time and Sports [database file]. 2008. International Social Survey Programme. Tel Aviv, Israel: The B.I. and Lucille Cohen Institute for Public Opinion Research, University of Tel Aviv.

Technical Appendix

Summary Description of Constructed Variables

1. Index of transformed variables

AUTORI2R (AUTORI2) – expectation of state authority
NACIO5 (NACIO) – provincial mentality - complex
NARIST05 (NARIST17) – plebeian mentality
PROVIN2R (PROVIN2) – provincial mentality - simple
TRANSFO5 (TRANSFOR) – transforming leadership style
TYPMO – type of preferred modernization path of our society

2. List of constructed and source variables

Variable names referencing the questionnaire are noticed for all source variables in both the elite and the general public surveys.

AUTORI2R (AUTORI2) – **expectation of state authority**
source variables:
elites: q4e, q51b
general public: q4e, q46b

NACIO5 (NACIO) – **provincial mentality – complex**
source variables:
elites: q7h, q17f, q17g, q51a
general public: q7h, q20f, q20g, q46a

NARIST05 (NARIST17) – **plebeian mentality**
source variables:
elites: neg(q4f), q27c, q51d, q51e
general public: neg(q4f), q27c, q46d, q46e

PROVIN2R (PROVIN2) – **provincial mentality** – **simple**
source variables:
elites: q7h , q51a
general public: q7h, q46a

TRANSFO5 (TRANSFOR) – **transforming leadership style**
source variables:
elites: q33a, neg(q33b), q33c, neg(33d), neg(q33f)
general public: q28a, neg(q28b), q28c, neg(q28d), neg(q28f)

TYPMO – **type of preferred modernization way of our society**
source variables:
elites: q8, q9
general public: q8, q9

All source variables were recoded in the following way in order to create constructed variables:

Answer	Value
strongly yes/strongly agree	+2
rather yes/rather agree	+1
do not know/no answer	0
rather no/rather disagree	−1
strongly no/strongly disagree	−2

3. Explanation of constructed variables and syntax (SPSS)

Elite AUTORI2, AUTORI2R
COMPUTE AUTORI2 = q4er + q51br .
EXECUTE .
RECODE
AUTORI2
(0=0) (3 thru 4=2) (1 thru 2=1) (−2 thru −1=−1) (−4 thru −3=−2) INTO AUTO-
RI2R .
EXECUTE .

Elite NACIO, NACIO5
COMPUTE NACIO = q7hr + q17fr + q17gr + q51ar .
EXECUTE .
RECODE
NACIO
(−8 thru −5=−2) (−4 thru −2=−1) (−1 thru 1=0) (2 thru 4=1) (5 thru 8=2)
INTO NACIO5 .

EXECUTE .

Elite NARIST17, NARIST05

COMPUTE NARIST17 = − q4fr + q27cr + q51dr + q51er .

EXECUTE .

RECODE

NARIST17

(−8 thru −6=−2) (−5 thru −3=−1) (−2 thru 2=0) (3 thru 5=1) (6 thru 8=2) INTO

NARIST05 .

EXECUTE .

Elite PROVIN2, PROVIN2R

COMPUTE PROVIN2 = q7hr + q51ar .

EXECUTE .

RECODE

PROVIN2

(0=0) (−4 thru −3=−2) (−2 thru −1=−1) (1 thru 2=1) (3 thru 4=2) INTO

PROVIN2R .

EXECUTE .

Elite TRANSFOR, TRANSFO5

COMPUTE TRANSFOR = q33ar − q33br + q33cr − q33dr − q33fr .

EXECUTE .

RECODE

transfor

(−10 thru −7=−2) (−6 thru −3=−1) (3 thru 6=1) (7 thru 10=2) (−2 thru

2=0) (ELSE=SYSMIS) INTO TRANSFO5 .

EXECUTE .

Elite TYPMO

IF (((q8 = 1) & (q9 = 3)) | ((q8 = 3) & (q9 = 1))) TYPMO = 1 .

EXECUTE .

IF (((q8 = 2) & (q9 = 4)) | ((q8 = 4) & (q9 = 2))) TYPMO = 3 .

EXECUTE .

IF (((q8 = 1) & (q9 = 2))

| ((q8 = 1) & (q9 = 4))

| ((q8 = 2) & (q9 = 1))

| ((q8 = 2) & (q9 = 3))

| ((q8 = 3) & (q9 = 2))

| ((q8 = 3) & (q9 = 4))

| ((q8 = 4) & (q9 = 1))

| ((q8 = 4) & (q9 = 3))

) TYPMO = 2 .

EXECUTE .
RECODE
TYPMO (MISSING=SYSMIS) .
EXECUTE .
FORMATS TYPMO (F8).
VARIABLE LABELS TYPMO "type of preferred modernization way of our society".
VALUE LABELS TYPMO
1.00000000000000 "technical"
2.00000000000000 "mixed"
3.00000000000000 "societal"

General Public AUTORI2, AUTORI2R
COMPUTE AUTORI2 = q4er + q46br .
EXECUTE .
RECODE
autori2
(0=0) (3 thru 4=2) (1 thru 2=1) (-2 thru -1=-1) (-4 thru -3=-2) INTO AUTORI2R .
EXECUTE .

General Public NACIO, NACIO5
COMPUTE NACIO = q7hr + q20fr + q20gr + q46ar .
EXECUTE .
RECODE
NACIO
(-8 thru -5=-2) (-4 thru -2=-1) (-1 thru 1=0) (2 thru 4=1) (5 thru 8=2) (ELSE=SYSMIS) INTO NACIO5 .
EXECUTE .

General Public NARIST17, NARIST05
COMPUTE NARIST17 = - q4fr + q27cr + q46dr + q46er .
EXECUTE .
RECODE
narist17
(-8 thru -6=-2) (-5 thru -3=-1) (-2 thru 2=0) (3 thru 5=1) (6 thru 8=2) INTO NARIST05 .
EXECUTE .
General Public PROVIN2, PROVIN2R
COMPUTE PROVIN2 = q7hr + q46ar .
EXECUTE .
RECODE

PROVIN2

(0=0) (−4 thru −3=−2) (−2 thru −1=−1) (1 thru 2=1) (3 thru 4=2) INTO PRO-VIN2R .

EXECUTE .

General Public TRANSFOR, TRANSFO5

COMPUTE TRANSFOR = q28ar − q28br + q28cr − q28dr − q28fr .

EXECUTE .

RECODE

transfor

(−10 thru −7=−2) (−6 thru −3=−1) (3 thru 6=1) (7 thru 10=2) (−2 thru 2=0) (ELSE=SYSMIS) INTO TRANSFO5 .

EXECUTE .

General Public TYPMO

IF (((q8 = 1) & (q9 = 3)) | ((q8 = 3) & (q9 = 1))) TYPMO = 1 .

EXECUTE .

IF (((q8 = 2) & (q9 = 4)) | ((q8 = 4) & (q9 = 2))) TYPMO = 3 .

EXECUTE .

IF (((q8 = 1) & (q9 = 2))

| ((q8 = 1) & (q9 = 4))

| ((q8 = 2) & (q9 = 1))

| ((q8 = 2) & (q9 = 3))

| ((q8 = 3) & (q9 = 2))

| ((q8 = 3) & (q9 = 4))

| ((q8 = 4) & (q9 = 1))

| ((q8 = 4) & (q9 = 3))

) TYPMO = 2 .

EXECUTE .

RECODE

TYPMO (MISSING=SYSMIS) .

EXECUTE .

FORMATS TYPMO (F8).

VARIABLE LABELS TYPMO "type of preferred modernization way of our society".

VALUE LABELS TYPMO

1.00000000000000 "technical"

2.00000000000000 "mixed"

3.00000000000000 "societal".

Name Index

Subject Index

Pavol Frič et al.

Czech Elites
and General Public:
Leadership, Cohesion,
and Democracy

Published by Charles University in Prague
Karolinum Press
Ovocný trh 3, 116 36 Praha 1
Prague 2010
Editor vice-rector Prof. PhDr. Ivan Jakubec, CSc.
Proofread by Clea McDonald
Layout Jan Šerých
Typeset by DTP Karolinum
Printed by Karolinum Press
First Edition

ISBN 978-80-246-1844-9